BIBLE POWER
FOR
SUCCESSFUL LIVING

By Norman Vincent Peale

By Norman Vincent Peale and Smiley Blanton

Bible POWER

FOR
SUCCESSFUL LIVING

Helping You Solve Everyday Problems

NORMAN VINCENT PEALE

and DONALD T. KAUFFMAN

PEALE CENTER FOR CHRISTIAN LIVING
66 E. MAIN STREET, PAWLING, N.Y. 12564-1409

Special Peale Center Edition

Library of Congress Cataloging-in-Publication Data

Peale, Norman Vincent, 1898-1993
   Bible power for successful living / helping you solve everyday problems / Norman Vincent Peale and Donald T. Kauffman.
       p. cm.
   ISBN 0-8007-1688-4
   1. Bible—Devotional use. 2. Bible—Reading. 3. Stress (Psychology)—Biblical teaching. 4. Success—Biblical teaching. 5. Peace of mind—Biblical teaching. I. Kauffman, Donald T. II. Title.
   BS617.8.P43   1993
   220'.07—dc20   93-3984

Contents

I am come that they might have life, and that they might have it more abundantly.

John 10:10

Beloved, I pray that you may prosper in all things and be in health, just as your soul prospers.

3 John 2 NKJV

*I*NTRODUCTION

*I*f you ever feel run-down or discouraged, if things aren't going right for you, perhaps your inner batteries need recharging.

Forty-one years ago I wrote in *The Power of Positive Thinking*, "This book is written to suggest techniques and to give examples which demonstrate that you do not need to be defeated by anything, that you can have peace of mind, improved health, and a never-ceasing flow of energy."[1] These may seem like astounding claims. Yet the reading of that book by fifteen million people in forty-five countries and the weaving of the phrase "positive thinking" into the warp and woof of modern life suggest these results are attainable.

One of the most important techniques outlined in *The Power of Positive Thinking* is the power of faith taught in the Bible. To develop that power, I recommend, "Saturate your mind with the great wisdom of the Bible."[2] If certain words and ideas from the Bible are made part of your thinking, they will work wonders in your life.

After decades of experience I am more confident than ever that the Bible's principles and prescriptions can help anyone anywhere live more effectively. But I find that many people bog down in their spiritual quest because the Bible baffles them. Others have a great deal of religious knowledge and may even read the Bible frequently but may not know how to utilize its ageless wisdom to solve their problems.

The Bible is not only a guide to spiritual life but also a very practical book. Its sixty-six books were written out of the hard experiences of life, by and about men and women facing great challenges and devastating difficulties: jealousy, ridicule, aging, childlessness, poverty, loneliness, hunger, sickness, homelessness, prison, and death. And God helped them solve their problems, as He helps us today.

This book is designed to show how to find in the Book of Books a never-ending source of practical power for happier, healthier, more successful living. Join me in this exciting adventure.

Norman Vincent Peale

HAPPIER, HEALTHIER LIVING

*O*ne night after a speech I stayed in a super-deluxe hotel—a huge place with picture windows, a swimming pool that looked practically Olympic size, and everything you could think of in terms of luxury and comfort. Upon my arrival, the manager had taken me to a beautiful suite of rooms where I found flowers and a basket of fruit. As I was expostulating about all this magnificence, the manager asked, "You know what is the most important thing in this room?"

I didn't have an inkling. He walked over to the desk and put his hand on the Bible that lay on it. "There," he said, "is the most important thing in this room."

Seeing my interest, the manager said, "I have a very personal love for this Book. It saved my life when I was close to losing it."

Then he told me of a string of disasters that had hit him all at once, as disasters sometimes do. His wife suddenly became ill and died within three hours. A promotion he anticipated went to another man. At the same time he discovered that his only son had gotten mixed up in some bad practices.

"Things got to a point where I was reeling," the hotel manager said. "One day I just put my head down on my desk and cried out: 'Lord, I'm licked. Please *help* me.'

"Soon afterward a strong urge came into my mind to read the Bible. I knew very little about that Book, but when I opened it, my eye fell on the statement from the Epistle to the Philippians: 'Be careful [anxious] for nothing; but in every thing by prayer and supplication with thanksgiving let your requests be made known unto God. And the peace of God, which passeth all understanding, shall keep your hearts and minds through Christ Jesus'" (Philippians 4:6–7).

What a magnificent formula for peace of mind! The hotel manager did exactly what this great Bible passage suggested. He tried to stop worrying and being overly anxious. He poured out his heart to the Lord, at the same time thanking Him for all the blessings that had filled his life. He visualized God's peace filling his heart and mind. And he repeated those two verses day after day, continuing to pray, give thanks, and trust. "The Lord received me," he said, "and gave me peace." And I could see why he felt as he did about the Bible, for through it he had learned to cope with some of life's roughest blows.

How to Benefit from the Bible

That is one way to benefit from the Bible: *Find a verse that speaks to your mind and make it part of your life.* I once walked into the office of an unusually successful businessman and noticed a Bible on his desk. "That is my Rule Book," he told me. "Whenever I don't know what to do, I find an answer in this Book."

While I was riding on the train from Philadelphia to New York after a speaking engagement some years ago, I took out my pocket Bible and began reading a favorite passage: Ephesians 6:10–17. I am fascinated by the way the apostle Paul shows how to fight the good fight of victorious faith. Our equipment, Paul explains, includes:

The breastplate of righteousness, to protect the heart.
The shoes of peace, to guide us into harmonious relationships.
The shield of faith, to ward off "the fiery darts of the wicked."
The helmet of salvation, to protect the mind against destructive thoughts.

The secret weapon of constant prayer.

And above all, "the sword of the Spirit, which is the word of God," to help us take the offensive against evil and negativism, and to win the battle.

As I studied that great passage, a voice said, "Pardon me, but may I ask what you are reading?"

I looked up to see a fellow passenger observing me with deep interest. I read the passage in Ephesians to him. He looked out the window for a long time, and I wondered if I had offended him in some way. I was relieved when he turned to me and said, "I believe that God sent you to ride with me today. Right now I am in the fight of my life. I am going to take 'the whole armor of God,' and with His help I am going to win."

A few weeks later I received a note from my fellow passenger: *Thank you for our time together on the train. Through the shield of faith and the sword of the Spirit I am winning my battle.*

One of the finest men I have ever known was Dr. Smiley Blanton, a psychiatrist who studied with Freud, founded the American Foundation of Religion and Psychiatry, and joined me in founding the Institutes of Religion and Health (now the Blanton Peale Institute). Smiley could turn to a favorite Scripture passage so quickly that it was obvious he knew the Bible like the back of his hand. He liked to tell of the mountain woman who lived alone in a cabin in the Tennessee hills during his childhood. "Aren't you lonely here, Mrs. Hood?" he asked her.

"No," she said, "I'm never lonely. God is with me." She pointed to the Bible near her. "If I ever feel lonely, I just read the Book and the promises in it."

Smiley Blanton considered no one hopeless, regardless of how bad or how great a failure he might seem. Probably the most important reason for his attitude was the teaching of the Bible. Smiley pointed out the case of Saul of Tarsus in the first century A.D. Saul persecuted the early Christians and even collaborated in the stoning of Stephen. But Saul met Jesus Christ and became Paul, who was perhaps the greatest figure in history except for Jesus. "If Paul could find forgiveness and a new life after all the evil he had done,"

Smiley said, "how much easier it should be for any of us to over-come our own failings through the infinite love of God."

Some of Smiley Blanton's favorite Scripture verses were:

> I will praise thee; for I am fearfully and wonderfully made (Psalm 139:14).
> Blessed are the poor in spirit: for theirs is the kingdom of heaven (Matthew 5:3).
> I sought the LORD and he heard me, and delivered me from all my fears (Psalm 34:4).
> Having done all . . . stand (Ephesians 6:13).

Blanton prescribed a sixteen-word formula for health and happiness from 1 Corinthians 13:13: "And now abideth faith, hope, and love, these three; but the greatest of these is love."

He was convinced, as I am, that believing in depth, facing the future with hope, using the power of Scripture, and living in love will guarantee the maximum in mental, spiritual, and even physical well-being.

Amazing Transformations

From my earliest years I have seen individuals change from fear, defeat, and self-loathing to victory and joy. I realized later that the transformations I had witnessed during my childhood resulted from my preacher father's faithful proclamation of the Bible's message of love and hope.

I myself was one of the changed ones, for I was plagued by feelings of insecurity and inferiority. I will never forget the summer afternoon I took a long walk with my father. He got me talking about my feeling that I had no ability and could never amount to anything.

At one point we sat down on two tree stumps while our little dog Tip ran about, puzzled, no doubt, by our stopping there. Father described the power of the inferiority complex to ruin a life. He said that psychiatric treatment could probably cure me, but none was available in our little town in Ohio. "However," he went on, "there is a Doctor right here who can cure any mental or emotional disease."

"Norman," my father asked me, "are you willing to let this Great Physician, Jesus Christ, heal you?"

When I said that I was, he knelt down with me by my stump. Tip came over and nuzzled my ear. Father committed me to Jesus Christ, and I surrendered myself and my inferiority feelings to Him. A strong sense of peace and confidence came over me. That old sense of inferiority sometimes returns, but I have learned that I can gain victory over it by the power of Christ and His words of assurance found in the Bible.

Indeed, from the Bible came my first strong impression of the living reality of Jesus. A Sunday school teacher once explained to our class how Jesus made a clear decision to go to Jerusalem, knowing full well that He would be arrested and killed there. She read the words from the Gospel of Luke: "He steadfastly set his face to go to Jerusalem" (9:51).

Suddenly those words gave me a picture of a rugged Master of Men marching fearlessly along a rocky road, confident and strong, clearly seeing that Jerusalem might mean the horrible prospect of death by crucifixion. The Bible came alive for me at that moment as Jesus Christ became a vibrant Friend whom I wanted to follow for the rest of my life.

And He is the heart and center of the Bible. If you want the key to the Bible's power, read the Gospels—Matthew, Mark, Luke, and John—and give yourself to the Man of Galilee. And He will walk beside you through every problem and difficulty you face.

Practical Daily Help

Many people turn to the Bible frequently simply because it gives them the practical help, energy, and know-how they need. Almost every happy, enthusiastic person I have ever known had a deep love for the Book, read it often, and drew on its inexhaustible resources for strength, guidance, and happiness.

Some people find in Scripture the help they need to get through devastating experiences. Terry Anderson, the last American hostage to be released after seven unimaginably awful years of captivity in Lebanon, said recently:

Constantly over the years, I found consolation and comfort in the Bible I was given in the first few weeks. Not other-world, "this is a test" kind of consolation, but comfort from the real immediate voices of people who had suffered greatly, and in ways that seemed so close to what I was going through. I read the Bible more than fifty times, cover to cover, in those first few years.[1]

When Rex Kern was star quarterback for the Ohio State Buckeyes, the Bible was an indispensable part of his life. During one of the Buckeyes' championship seasons, he said, "I read the Bible so I can receive added strength when it is most sorely needed."[2]

> **Men and women today are finding that the Bible's ancient wisdom is not only abreast of the times but ahead of them, a peerless source of practical inspiration.**

Businessman Stanley Ford wondered what wisdom the Bible might offer while he was searching for better methods of business management. He discovered, in the Old and New Testaments, dozens of workable, "new, two-thousand-year-old ideas" for business efficiency and success. "Much of the advice in the Bible," Ford said, "has been especially beneficial to me. Applying the Christian ethic to corporate concerns results in a satisfying and productive life and profits everybody."[3]

Don't Feel Intimidated by the Bible

At this point you may feel intimidated. You may look at the Bible as a book of rules hopelessly hard to understand or follow. You may have been told that you should read the Bible every day, and you may even be doing this with little to show for it. Or you may feel that the Bible is too ancient to be of value in our modern life with all its problems and complexities.

I am not going to try to answer all these difficulties. Let me just say in passing that there must be a reason why the Bible is the best-selling book in the history of the world and why it has been "the Book" for millions of people for thousands of years. Perhaps the writings of Marx or Lenin or Chairman Mao competed as best sellers a few years ago, but today millions of former Communists have turned completely away from their threadbare former beliefs and are asking instead for Bibles! Men and women today are finding that the Bible's ancient wisdom is not only abreast of the times but ahead of them, a peerless source of practical inspiration.

The Bible was written not so much to point out our mistakes (although there is value in honestly facing our failures) as to inspire us to better, happier living. Used positively, as I try to show in this book, the Bible leads to a unique sense of self-esteem and power.

The Bible can indeed be hard to understand, particularly if you read a centuries-old translation such as the King James or Douay Version. Beautiful and valuable as such versions are, their wording comes from the era of Shakespeare or earlier, and not many of us are adept at understanding Shakespeare's terminology.

So if you find the Bible difficult to read, let me offer a few suggestions.

1. *Buy a contemporary translation of the Bible.* Note, for example, the common-sense power and immediacy of J. B. Phillips' modern English translation of the passage quoted earlier in this chapter from Philippians 4:6–7:

> Don't worry over anything whatever... tell God every detail of your needs in thankful prayer, and the peace of God, which surpasses human understanding, will keep constant guard over your hearts and minds as they rest in Christ Jesus.

There are numerous excellent modern translations and paraphrases of Scripture. The Revised Standard Version, the New International Version, The New English Bible, Today's English Version (sometimes called The Good News Bible), the New King James Version, The Living Bible, and the recent Contemporary English Version are a few you should be able to find in most bookstores.

One day in the 1960s two hippies were looking at a copy of Today's English Version, a version of the Bible published by the American Bible Society. One hippie said in amazement, "Looks like the Bible, man, but it can't be. I dig it!" With a Bible in today's language, you too will "dig" the timeless words in a new way.

2. *Begin with the Gospels, the Letters (Epistles) of the New Testament, or perhaps the Psalms or Proverbs.* As you read, look for

a verse or passage that speaks to your need. Write it down, memorize it, and make it part of your life. As such a passage sinks down into your mind, it will permeate your subconscious and produce marvelous changes in all your relationships.

While the Russian empire was still a totalitarian menace, Stalin's daughter Svetlana, in her thirty-fifth year, began to sense the reality of a spiritual world. She said, "I looked for the words to express this new sensation and found it in the Psalms of David. Since then I have found nothing that better expressed the Higher, Eternal Life . . . Nowhere have I found words more powerful than those in the Psalms. Their fervid poetry cleanses one, gives one strength, brings hope in moments of darkness."[4]

3. *Eventually branch out into other parts of the Bible, such as the Acts, Genesis, and Isaiah.* Again, look for "power verses" or "wisdom verses" and make them part of your life. Repeat them to yourself first thing each morning and last thing at night. Share them with someone else who needs a lift. (They will return with greater power and wisdom to your own life.)

I once collected many of the great verses of the Bible, with a few comments on each, in two little booklets entitled *Thought Conditioners* and *Spirit Lifters.*[5] These have been for years the most widely distributed booklets of the Peale Center for Christian Living. The idea behind *Thought Conditioners* is that just as air conditioning refreshes the atmosphere of a room, the promises and principles of God in the Bible will refresh and renew your life.

A letter recently came to my offices in Pawling, New York, from an individual in Maine who described this booklet as "a kind of short Bible" that had completely changed his life. *Thought Conditioners* and *Spirit Lifters* are no substitute for the Bible, but the Scriptures in both have had a powerful effect on a great many people.

4. *Concentrate not so much on intellectual mastery of Bible facts and details as on applying God's wisdom to your everyday problems.* For example, suppose you are troubled by fear and worry. (If so, you are not alone—Dr. Smiley Blanton called fear and anxiety "the great modern plague," and it can be just as devastating as the plagues of the Middle Ages.) Apply to your fear and worry this remarkable prescription:

Peace I leave with you, my peace I give unto you: not as the world giveth, give I unto you. Let not your heart be troubled, neither let it be afraid.

John 14:27

Let those words of Jesus, the Master Psychiatrist, sink deep into your mind and heart. If you will repeat them often and think of the deep peace they represent, you will find that they will drive out all the tension.

5. *Approach the Bible positively.* Ken Winslow, a fellow worker at the Peale Center for Christian Living, recently remarked that people may shy away from the Bible because they read it with a negative attitude. You can look for flaws in the Bible; if you do, you can come up with what look like inconsistencies, contradictions, and so on. Certain scholars have majored in this and have given the unfortunate impression that the Bible is full of "mistakes."

In the same way anyone could examine a painting by Rembrandt and point out places where his brush may have slipped, his colors are too dark, or his straight lines are irregular. But this is not the way to get inspiration from a work of art! Today a great many Bible scholars are acknowledging the mistake of approaching the Bible in a similar fashion and are finding anew, as millions of people have found in every generation, the power and relevancy of the one book that can be called the Book of Books.

It is possible to be "thrown" by the Bible's many references to sin and punishment. But we must remember that, while this Book challenges us to the highest moral and ethical standards, it is essentially a revelation of the amazing grace and boundless love of God, exemplified above all through the words and work of Jesus Christ.

The very word Gospel means "good news" and is so translated in many present-day translations of Holy Writ. And the word Law, or Torah, in the Old Testament, Hebrew scholars tell me, means "revelation"—basically, the revelation of the love of God and His desire to give each one of His billions of children the best possible life, now and forever.

So do not begin your Bible reading looking for negatives. Search instead for its many references to God's love and forgiveness, its examples of great living, its wisdom for handling problems, and its promises and principles of joyous, abundant living.

6. *Approach the Bible with an open mind.* You may ask, "How do I know the Bible will help me?" You cannot prove in advance that it will. But you could approach it with an open mind, scientifically, the same way a scientist approaches a problem.

What is the scientific method? It is to look at a problem honestly, objectively, without preconceived ideas as to whether one method or another can or cannot solve it, and to find a hypothesis that fits it and stands up to repeated tests for verification.

Let me illustrate with the organization Alcoholics Anonymous (AA). Many businesses and hospitals encourage and recommend this organization. If someone told you that you could master an oppressive habit by going to meetings where no one seemed to be in charge, where the members knew each other only by their first names and talked mostly about their failures, and where each meeting ended with the Lord's Prayer, wouldn't you be a little skeptical? Yet Alcoholics Anonymous works. It has done far more than any other organization or technique I know of in releasing alcoholics from their bondage. In fact, it is so successful that other groups with problems have copied its format and Russian leaders have asked for help in setting up such groups in their country.

The simple fact is that AA is uniquely effective. And another simple and equally indisputable fact is that the Bible works—for the betterment and blessing of millions of men and women.

7. *Read the Bible expectantly.* Life usually gives you what you look for. A chaplain of New York's Bowery Mission once said, "When you read the Bible, look for a precept, a principle, or a promise." That is good advice. In almost every passage of Scripture you will find either a precept (a suggestion for guidance), a principle (an illustration of how to cope with a particular situation), or a promise of God's abundant blessing.

"When all else fails," some wag has said, "read the instructions." It makes no more sense to ignore the precepts of the Bible than to buy a car and ignore the manufacturer's directions for its use. If you fail to keep oil in the motor or water in the radiator, you can reap a lot of grief!

The Bible is filled with marvelous stories of men and women who were basically like you and me. What happened to these people and how they faced their crises and problems shows the Bible's wisdom for our own lives today. Their examples and the clear principles of Scripture, such as those in the Sermon on the Mount and the Ten Commandments, are extremely important for better, happier living.

Scripture is also filled with wonderful promises from our heavenly Father. Most of these promises were given to particular individuals in specific situations, but every one has a spiritual meaning for us. Everything in the Bible was "written for our admonition," or guidance (1 Corinthians 10:11). And "all the promises of God in him [Christ] are yea, and in him Amen, unto the glory of God" (2 Corinthians 1:20). Jesus is God's "Yes" to every promise.

8. *Use the Bible intelligently.* A friend in New York City, Dr. John Sutherland Bonnell, once told of a parishioner who felt that his sermons were too intellectual. "Pastor," the parishioner said, "when I come to church I want to unscrew my head and leave it under the pew." Most of us don't enjoy sermons that are too weighty, but God gave us our heads for a good reason. The more mental effort you put into Scripture study, the more help you will receive.

To understand the Bible better, and to get more benefit from it, you will profit from using a good Bible dictionary, a concordance, and a Bible handbook. You can probably find these in your church or in a religious bookstore. A Bible dictionary provides helpful information about Bible subjects, personalities, places, and events. A concordance is a sort of dictionary that tells you where to find various Bible passages. (You may find it helpful to ask your pastor or someone familiar with concordances how to use one effectively.) A Bible handbook gives important information about various aspects of the Bible: the background, the author, the purpose, and so forth. As you go deeper into the Scriptures, you can find valuable help in commentaries on individual books.

Approaching the Bible with such helps is even more important than studying music appreciation for greater enjoyment of the classics. The more you know, the more help you can get from whatever you are studying.

Many people have found great blessing by simply opening the Bible and reading. But this can be puzzling and frustrating until we learn why something was written and what it meant to the original writers. The background, which can be gleaned from one of the reference books mentioned above, can provide important preparation for receiving the spiritual benefits of a verse or passage.

9. *Read with the heart and imagination.* For the most benefit from the Bible, read it with both your mind and your heart open to what God wants to say to you. When we do this, He can apply His truth to our problems and our total lives in a special way, for the Scriptures are "spiritually discerned" (1 Corinthians 2:13–14).

To read without spiritual discernment is like trying to see something through a heavy veil. Opening our hearts to the Lord takes the veil away (2 Corinthians 3:16). As we look for the spiritual meaning of the Bible for our daily needs, a wonderful thing happens. We are transformed into God's very image (2 Corinthians 3:18). Our lives and interests are changed into the mature, loving, spiritually discerning personality of the Lord Himself.

So read the Bible with both sides of your brain, to put it in modern psychological terms—both thoughtfully and imaginatively. When you read the Gospels, try to picture Jesus, see His face, and hear His strong, caring voice. Visualize the people around Him and try to feel what is happening to them.

Then go a step further. Picture yourself there in the presence of Jesus. What is He saying to you? What does He want you to do? How can you follow Him and demonstrate His love to the next person you see?

A shepherd in Israel wrote centuries ago about the Bible: "How sweet are thy words unto my taste! . . . Through thy precepts I get understanding . . . Thy word is a lamp unto my feet, and a light unto my path" (Psalm 119:103–105). Give the Bible an honest chance, and you too will find delight, wisdom, power, and guidance through its pages.

For maximum benefit from the Bible:

1. Approach it with an open mind.
2. Read it expectantly. Ask God for guidance and believe He is giving it.

3. As you read, look for a sentence or passage that speaks to your mind and heart, and make it part of your life.
4. Try reading a contemporary translation such as Today's English Version.
5. Begin with the Gospels, the Epistles, the Proverbs, or the Psalms, and eventually branch out into other Scriptures.
6. Read the Bible intelligently. Find out who is speaking, where, to whom, and why.
7. Read it creatively, with your heart and imagination, and look for its wise guidance.
8. Apply what you read to your everyday problems.
9. Give the Bible's wisdom an opportunity to revitalize your life.

HOW TO TACKLE A GIANT PROBLEM

2

_A_re you facing a problem so huge there seems to be no possible solution? If so, you are not alone.

Consider the problem little David had three thousand years ago when he faced the ten-foot giant Goliath. (You can find the whole fascinating story in the Old Testament Book of 1 Samuel, chapter 17.)

Shepherd boy David was apparently too young to join his brothers when they marched off to defend their land against the hordes of ravaging Philistines. But he must have jumped for joy when his father asked him to take some bread, parched corn, and cheese to his brothers on the battlefront. He couldn't believe it when he saw the giant Goliath parading on a hilltop and challenging any Hebrew to a duel, one on one.

"Choose a man to fight me," the giant yelled across the space between the armies. "If he kills me," he continued in effect, "we Philistines will be your slaves. But if I win, you Hebrews will become our slaves.

"I defy the armies of Israel this day!" shouted Goliath, the sun glinting off his brass coat of mail and his enormous spear and shield. (His coat of mail alone weighed over a hundred pounds.) "Give me a man," he said, "that we may fight!"

David's spirit was aflame with indignation when he saw this affront to his people and his God. The Philistines were Israel's worst enemies. Tall and well-organized, they had a monopoly on the manufacture of iron and struck fear into their opponents with their chariots, swords, and spears, all made on their own forges. (The Israelites had to buy their military weapons from the Philistines and then had to come to one of the Philistine towns just to get them sharpened.)

David also opposed the Philistines because he loved the one true God, while they worshiped a host of idol gods and goddesses, one of the chief being Astarte, or Ashtoreth, the "queen of heaven" who was infamous for the lewd sexual practices and ritual prostitution that accompanied her worship.

"Who is this uncircumcised Philistine," David asked, "that he should defy the armies of the living God?" *Why doesn't someone fight him?* he must have asked himself. *How can they stand there and accept these insults?* This youngest brother had a true fighting spirit—ready to risk his life for God and country.

When King Saul learned of David's zeal, he offered him his own armor, but it was too big for the boy—and he didn't need it. He had his own trusted weapons: a slingshot and five smooth pebbles.

Seeing this little boy coming to fight him, Goliath must have roared with laughter. "Come to me," he shouted, "and I'll feed your flesh to the birds and your bones to the beasts of the field."

But David knew he had a secret weapon deadlier than his slingshot. "You come to me with a sword, and a spear, and a shield," David called out as he advanced. "But I come to you in the name of the Lord of hosts . . . This day the Lord will deliver you into my hand, and I will take off your head. It is the carcasses of the Philistines that will be food for the birds and beasts!

"Then," David shouted his final challenge, "everyone will know that the battle is the Lord's, and He will deliver you into our hands."

The next thing Goliath knew was the impact of a small stone driven at enormous speed to a spot between his eyes. He sank to the ground. David ran forward, drew the giant's sword from his scabbard and cut off his head. The amazed Philistines fled, the Israelite soldiers followed them, and soon they had captured back what the enemy had stolen. And the whole nation rejoiced.

You Can Conquer the Biggest Problem

David's contest with Goliath points the way to conquering the giant problems that come to us. The next time you face one of these, think of how David beat that ten-foot giant. Remember to:

1. *Keep cool.* The Israelite soldiers were awed by the size of the brutish Goliath, who filled the whole Israelite army with fear. But David, who was considered too young to fight, did not let fear destroy his ability to size up the situation. In facing your own problems, do not let your mind get overheated. A cool head is the most valuable possession you can have.

2. *Keep your heart open to the possibilities God may have in store for you.* Awesome as Goliath must have looked, David kept the eyes of his heart fixed on something far greater—the glory and power of the living Lord.

The Bible tells us much about the power of the human heart. For a clearer understanding of this, turn with me to Deuteronomy 6:5, "And thou shalt love the LORD thy God with all thine heart, and all thy soul, and with all thy might."

Perhaps it will be helpful to visualize this by thinking of three concentric circles superimposed over the figure of a person. The circle at the very center represents the heart, the inmost being. A circle surrounding that is the soul, our spiritual essence. The outer circle stands for our strength, our total energies and deeds.

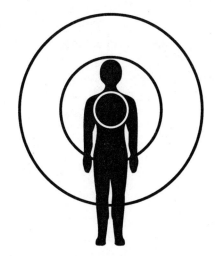

In other words, in the Bible "heart" does not mean the organ that pumps blood through our system, but what that organ represents:

the center and source of our life and thought and courage and emotions. Just as our physical heart is the center of the human torso, so the heart, as the Bible usually speaks of it, is the dynamic center of our thinking and planning and imagination. "For as he thinketh in his heart, so is he" (Proverbs 23:7). God gave Solomon "a wise and an understanding heart" (1 Kings 3:12). Out of our hearts come our thoughts, desires, and plans (Hebrews 4:12). The Bible teaches that all wrong deeds begin as thoughts from our hearts (Mark 7:21) and therefore constantly reminds us to ask the Lord to control and direct our deepest inner selves (Psalm 51:10). Only then are we prepared to meet whatever comes.

3. *Be humbly confident that with God's help, nothing need defeat you.* David knew he was an expert shot with the sling. He was sure he could conquer Goliath (1 Samuel 17:37). We can have the same confidence (Mark 9:23).

Turn for a moment now to another conflict with giants, beginning in Numbers 13:1. The children of Israel stood at the very threshold of the Promised Land. The blessings God had for them there were so abundant that it took two men to carry one cluster of grapes (verse 23). The leader, Caleb, said, "Let us go up at once, and possess it; for we are well able to overcome it" (verse 30).

But the majority of the Israelites' search committee thought of all the negatives they could imagine. You will find them listed in Numbers 13:28–33. Instead of seeing the possibilities in the Promised Land, as Caleb did, they concentrated on the walled cities, the number of different peoples living there, the difficulties, and above all, the giants: "We were in our own sight as grasshoppers" (verse 33).

Now, enormous as some of those giants may have been, surely these men were letting their fears distort the situation out of all recognition. The largest giant on record is Goliath. Even though he was ten feet tall, the Israelites were certainly far bigger than grasshoppers in comparison!

Because the people of God took that fearful, negative attitude, He did not let them into the Promised Land for another forty years (Numbers 14:26–34). And we can shape our future by whether we face our problems in fear or in confident faith.

4. *Refuse to be discouraged.* David, the little youngest brother, was "squelched" first by his brother Eliab (1 Samuel 17:28), then by King Saul (verse 33), and finally by Goliath (verses 42–44). David knew what he had accomplished when a bear and a lion had attacked his sheep, and he knew that the Lord who had delivered him then would stand by him still (verse 37). We have God's promise that we need never fear anything because He will always stand by us (Psalm 27:1; Isaiah 41:10).

5. *Use your head.* King Saul offered David his own armor to fight Goliath, but David dared to differ. He refused to fight the way the king wanted, for he had his own plan of attack (1 Samuel 17:38–40). He believed in God, and he very carefully thought out the way to bring the giant down.

Your mind is such a magnificent instrument that science has barely probed the surface of its tremendous powers. Dr. Steven Greer of the Royal Marsden Hospital in England says that the human mind can make the difference between life and death. Dr. Greer studied thirty-nine women who had had mastectomies. He says in the videotape series *The Mind* that their attitudes correlated highly with their survival.

"The women who had a positive attitude," declares Dr. Greer, "had the best outcome." He reports that ten years after the mastectomies, these women were twice as likely to be still alive as the women who let the disease overwhelm them.

The videotape "Pain and Healing" in this series presents one of these women, Rachel Beals, who was told she had only twelve months to live after she lost a breast and one lung collapsed. Refusing to give in, Rachel resumed her teaching career and took up sports. She testifies:

> I'm sure I would not be here now if I hadn't developed this absolute attitude that I was going to win. I don't think you are just a machine. You have a body and soul and spirit, and you must utilize them. If you cut off the mind, which is a very powerful instrument within your body, you're losing a whole spectrum of what can make you better.

If you can give yourself a migraine headache from being uptight, why can't you use your mind to make your body feel good? I'm not cured yet. I'm going to be because I'm determined to be.[1]

6. *Expect the best but be prepared for the worst.* What if David's pebble had missed Goliath? He had four more stones as backup. David knew he was fallible and therefore he was a brilliant leader and a person God could use.

7. *Trust God.* David was confident the Lord would give him the victory. He did his best and committed the situation to God. "Having done all . . . stand" (Ephesians 6:13). There comes a point when we can do nothing more. That is the time to relax and trust. Remember, "greater is he that is in you, than he that is in the world" (1 John 4:4). "He which hath begun a good work in you will perform [complete] it until the day of Jesus Christ" (Philippians 1:6).

The Power of Your Mind

The Bible says a great deal about the importance of right thinking. Evil thinking grieved the Lord and brought about the disaster of the flood (Genesis 6:5–6). The Bible tells us, "Wisdom is the principal thing; therefore get wisdom" (Proverbs 4:7). "Through wisdom is a house builded; and by understanding it is established" (Proverbs 24:3).

The thinking person who loves knowledge stands in contrast to the brutish man of Proverbs 12:1; the thoughts of the righteous are right, while the counsels (thoughts and advice) of the wicked lead to disaster (Proverbs 12:5). "The mind of the righteous ponders how to answer" (Proverbs 15:28 RSV).

After Jesus healed a man with an unclean spirit, he was found "clothed, and in his right mind" (Mark 5:15). The Savior constantly appealed to people's intelligence, asking questions and telling stories or parables that demanded honest thinking. He often asked His hearers what they thought (Matthew 17:25; 21:28; Luke 10:36).

The New Testament tells us to bring "into captivity every thought to the obedience of Christ" (2 Corinthians 10:5). God invites, "Let this mind be in you, which was also in Christ Jesus" (Philippians 2:5).

Write out and repeat to yourself the great words of Romans 12:1–2, underlining the words *reasonable service* and *transformed by the renewing of your mind.* These powerful verses teach that we can become completely remade through renewed thought processes.

Solve Your Problems Creatively

One of the most profound and important truths in the Bible is this: "God created man in his own image" (Genesis 1:27). Our heavenly Father has put His divine image within us all. What is that image? Doubtless it has numerous facets, from love and sensitivity to imagination and wisdom, but surely one of its most thrilling aspects is creativity. Our Creator God made us like Himself, thus enabling us to be creative too.

You may be thinking, "I'm not creative." Never think that! God the Creator has made you like Himself. The Bible makes clear that we have all sinned and marred that image, but it is renewed and recreated in every believer (Colossians 3:9–10). The *Good News Bible* translates these verses:

> You have put off the old self with its habits and have put on the new self. This is the new being which God, its Creator, is constantly renewing in his own image, in order to bring you to a full knowledge of himself.

Say to yourself: *I will no longer let my old defeatist self control me. I now say good-bye to the bad habits of my old self. Henceforth I will consciously put on my new creative self, the same way I put on a new dress or a new suit. Today and every day I will let God renew my heart and will. I will free His creative energy within me to begin solving my problems.*

Underline the words *renewed in knowledge* in Colossians 3:10 in your Bible. You may have a problem that seems to have you stumped. God wants to renew your thinking about it!

How do you face problems creatively? Creativity is first of all getting a mental vision of the solution. Long before God created the world, He visualized you and me and loved us. Look up Ephesians 1:3–4 in your Bible, which tells us exactly that. And He has already "blessed us with all spiritual blessings!" Furthermore, God created us to do the good works He has planned for us, ordaining long ago "that we should walk in them" (Ephesians 2:10).

Another thing the Bible tells us is: To create is often to make something new out of something we already have. God must have made the world out of nothing, but when He created men and women, He formed them out "of the dust of the ground" (Genesis 2:7). The scientist Slosson points out that God is still doing this. Out of the ground grow all living things, and when we eat our breakfast cereal—or anything else—He is using the elements in the earth to renew the cells of our bodies and brains.

So creativity can be using something old in a new way, or combining two or three things to make something new. Long ago someone must have noticed that a heavy object moves more easily when it rests on small stones or saplings. One of our ancestors may have cut such saplings into short lengths to make wheels, and the first wagons were created! Later someone put a motor into a wagon and it became an "auto-mobile," a self-propelled vehicle.

But none of this happened by chance. The Spirit of God is the spirit of creativity. The Lord gave Bezalel and other craftsmen the skills to create the beautiful furnishings of the tabernacle from gold, silver, special woods, and precious stones (Exodus 31:1–11). He gave King David skills not only in leadership but also in creating marvelous music and poetry. How impoverished we would be without the Psalms of David, the Epistles wrought out of the struggles and dreams of the apostle Paul, and indeed all great literature and art. The Creator will give you, too, the creative ability to handle any situation in which you find yourself.

Conquering Your Difficulties

Let us apply some of these Bible principles to your own special problems.

1. *Believe God will give you new ideas and solutions as you turn to Him.* Trust your faithful Creator to give you the thoughts and even the words you need (Matthew 10:19). Turn to Isaiah 57:19

and underline the words "I create the fruit of the lips." Also underline Proverbs 16:1.

One of the finest men I ever knew was Harry Bullis. A tall, thin,
shy adolescent, he felt totally discouraged because of his deep inferiority complex. While Harry was moping around the house one
day, his mother said to him: "Harry, I want you to go take a good
walk in the woods. Then tell God all about your problems. But don't
leave until He tells you what to do. Listen real hard till you hear
Him speak."

Harry did that. He walked in the woods with his dog until his
mind began to clear. Then he sat down on a big log, his dog beside
him, and poured out to God all the misery in his mind and heart.
Every once in a while his dog would look up at him with love in his
eyes as if to say, "Don't you mind, Harry, I love you." When Harry
was through praying he listened.

And just as clearly as he ever heard anything in his life, Harry
heard a voice—not outwardly, but inwardly—"Harry, throw your
head back, stand on your feet, and be a man. Believe in yourself. Believe in Me. Follow Me all the way and I will lead you to
a good life."

Harry Bullis obeyed that voice. He became a flour mill executive
and an outstanding Christian, a big, jovial man who did many wonderful things for others. And in all the years that followed, when
he was beset with problems, he would get by himself, talk it all out,
and listen until the answer came.

Write down these great words from Psalm 46:10: "Be still, and
know that I am God." Sit quietly until you feel the loving peace of
God enfold you, and wait for Him to guide you.

If you clear your mind, read the Bible, and earnestly listen to what
God says, He will show you a creative new answer to your problem.

> **Positive thinking always searches through the worst pos-
> sible situation until it finds the best possible outcome.**

2. *Take a new look at your problem.* You may see it in a new light.

A widow in Connecticut was giving all she could to her church
when it burned down. The church officials decided to rebuild it and

asked each member to make two pledges: the usual annual commitment and an additional pledge toward a new building. Ella (as I will call her) knew she could not give any more out of her limited income. But she asked herself whether there was not some new way she could contribute. Having a talent for sewing, she pledged in faith a thousand dollars toward the new building. Then, collecting clothing and other materials that had been discarded, she set about repairing and selling them. During the next two years Ella made over a thousand dollars, which she contributed toward the new church.

3. *Look for the opportunities before you.* Positive thinking always searches through the worst possible situation until it finds the best possible outcome. Go back over your lifetime and see if this hasn't been true in your case. So often what seems terrible contains the seeds of something wonderful. And you will find wonderful opportunities in your problems if you face them creatively.

A mother once took her eight-year-old son to a concert by the noted pianist Paderewski. She thought her boy had some musical talent and would benefit from the concert. Imagine her consternation when, just before Paderewski appeared, the little boy ran up onto the stage and began to pound out "Chopsticks" on the grand piano. And imagine how embarrassed the pianist might have felt!

But when Paderewski appeared he went to the piano, sat down by the little boy and put his arms around him. Whispering to him to continue, he improvised a brilliant accompaniment to the childish tune. The listeners burst into applause.

Whatever happens in your life, look for God's creative ways to respond so that instead of embarrassment and hurt, there can be an inspired solution. Don't waste your time lamenting what cannot be changed. The new possibilities God has for you may be far better than what you had before. God never closes one door without opening another.

With His ever-present help, you can meet the biggest problems confidently and victoriously.

When you face a giant problem:

1. Keep cool.
2. Be open to God's creative possibilities.

3. Maintain a humbly confident attitude.
4. Refuse to be discouraged.
5. Use your head.
6. Expect the best—but be prepared for the worst.
7. Trust God to see you through.
8. Believe the Lord will give you new ideas and solutions.
9. Seize the opportunities that come—for they surely will.
10. Remember that no problem is too big for almighty God.

MOVE UP OUT OF THE DARKNESS

3

*I*f you are struggling with a problem so difficult that everything looks pitch dark, let me assure you I can empathize. There are times when some of us feel like the ancient psalm writer who cried out, "Thou hast laid me in the lowest pit, in darkness, in the deeps" (Psalm 88:6).

And there is often a reason for feeling that way. This is not going to be a Pollyanna-ish chapter telling you simply, "Cheer up and look on the bright side," for you may have problems so deep you cannot see a bright side. There are times when anyone may face such a disappointment, or such a hard blow, that everything looks hopeless. What I want to do is to bring from God's Word some guidance on how to face the darkness that may engulf you when everything seems to go wrong.

A well-known physician once made a valuable observation about the many patients he knew for whom life had become an almost intolerable burden. He said: "I believe that people would be healthier, live longer, and do better work if they could learn to handle their disappointments skillfully." Disappointments come to everyone. We cannot escape them. What we can do is handle them well, so that we can make the best of whatever happens.

Please take a new look with me at the very first words of the Bible. Read these words from Genesis 1:1–4 with creative imagination:

> In the beginning God created the heaven and the earth. And the earth was without form, and void; and darkness was upon the face of the deep. And the Spirit of God moved upon the face of the waters. And God said, Let there be light: and there was light. And God saw the light, that it was good.

Note carefully: Back at the beginning of the universe the whole earth was formless, empty, covered with darkness. The words remind us of our own lives when we are so overwhelmed that we cannot see any light. At such moments everything seems chaotic, disordered, empty, meaningless.

What can we do?

God Is Always There, Even in the Darkness

When things look pitch black, be aware that God is present even in your darkness. The universe began in darkness!

A little boy was afraid of the dark. Then, one night, he decided to face his fears. He lived in a small village before electric lights were everywhere; the only light in his house was the feeble glow of a kerosene lamp in the living room.

Summoning his courage, Donny crept out the back door of his house into the dark. There was no moon; even the stars were hidden behind clouds, and the darkness was nearly total.

But as Donny stood there in his backyard, slowly his eyes adjusted to the darkness. He could sense, more by touch and smell than by sight, the flower garden and the raspberry patch close to the house. He heard a breeze sighing in the trees overhead. And he said to himself, *There is nothing to be afraid of in the dark!*

In the Bible, darkness often represents evil, while God and goodness are represented by light. But God created the dark as well as the light! He was in the heart of the deep darkness that surrounded Mount Sinai at the giving of the Ten Commandments (Exodus 20:21). And when darkness blotted out the sun for three hours on the day when Jesus was dying on a cross, surely God was never more present.

Not only is God present in the darkness, but He is actively working there. The Book of Genesis continues that in the primordial darkness, "The Spirit of God moved" (1:2). No matter how difficult your situation, no matter how deep your darkness, always know that God is present and is moving to bring about the best possible result.

Dr. John Claypool, a great minister, once spoke about the problem of seemingly unanswered prayer. He told of the agony he had often felt as he prayed for his only sister, Marie, who had been suffering for years from bouts with mental illness.

Sometimes Marie seemed about to fall apart emotionally. John prayed again and again, "Lord, please don't let Marie break down." Then one day he received a telephone call from Marie's employers in another state. They told him that his sister had suffered a total nervous breakdown and that they were sending her home by plane.

Marie was so disoriented that when the plane arrived she didn't seem to know how to get off. When she was helped off, she did not recognize her parents. She had totally collapsed. She had to be hospitalized for months. For a long period she did not even know her own name.

The one thing John Claypool had feared, and had prayed would not happen, happened. It seemed as though God had completely disregarded his fervent prayers. Then this minister remembered that God answers prayer in three ways: yes, no, or wait awhile.

Out of that collapse something else happened. After everything fell apart for Marie, she began to reorganize her personality in a brand-new way.

Marie had responded negatively to her parents' training. She had never married, and she blamed that fact on her upbringing. John had sensed within her a deep resentment that she had never admitted and dealt with. All this had led to her emotional breakdown.

Now, however, Marie came to herself, integrated on a higher and healthier level than ever before. She displayed a quiet acceptance of life and of the fact that she might never marry. Slowly she came back to normality and was able to take a job. At the end of that year, at a Christmas party, Marie met a social worker who also had never

> ### The fact is that God is often most active
> ### when the darkness seems deepest.

married because he had given most of his life to the care of his aged
mother. The two fell in love, and next Thanksgiving they were married. "Now," reports Dr. Claypool, "Marie is happier, more in touch
with wholeness, than I have ever seen her."

In John's and Marie's darkness God was working. Out of that
darkness came light and healing. And it can come for anyone who
believes.

The fact is that God is often most active when the darkness
seems deepest. The author of Psalm 139 realized this. "Whither
shall I go from thy spirit?" he asked. "If I make my bed in hell,
behold, thou art there. If I take the wings of the morning, and dwell
in the uttermost parts of the sea; even there shall thy hand lead me,
and thy right hand shall hold me" (verses 7–10). If there are
moments when you feel that you are living in hell, do not forget
that even there God is with you—holding you and leading you.

Often God moves more slowly than we like. But the best things
in life, from an oak tree to a good marriage, usually take time. The
Book of Exodus records that the Jewish people were slaves in
Egypt for four hundred years. Finally Moses was born and determined to set his people free. But his first efforts led to disaster, and
he was eighty years old before God was able to use him to liberate
His people. (The story is in the first chapters of the Book of Exodus.) Then, centuries more went by before the Messiah was born
in a little town called Bethlehem and joy came to the world. No
doubt you and I would like to work more quickly than that, but
when God takes His time, whether with a tree or a life, glorious
results come! He is always moving in our lives, whether we realize
it or not.

Agnes Sanford, the author of some remarkable books on prayer
and healing, was visiting a veterans' hospital when she came across
a young man whose leg had been filled with shrapnel in battle and
had not healed. He had developed the bone disease osteomyelitis
and his leg broke so often that he was finally put in the ward for
incurable veterans.

Agnes talked and prayed with John, the veteran, in her own gifted way, and in a few weeks his leg was healed sufficiently for him to be discharged from the hospital.

Some months later, however, when she was making another visit to the same hospital, she came across the young soldier in another ward. He was in traction. "My leg broke again," John said. "I was discouraged for a few days, but then I figured maybe there was something else God wanted me to know."

There was. Talking with him, Agnes found that just before the leg had broken this last time, John had been filled with such rage that he had picked up a typewriter and smashed it onto the floor. And she found that he often had these uncontrollable rages.

Then she discovered something else about John. During his childhood in Germany, both the boy's father and mother had been carried off to Nazi concentration camps, and while John was growing up the Hitler youth gangs had ridiculed him and thrown stones at him. All John could do was take it—but he carried these searing memories inside.

Agnes felt that some people have such destructive memories that they are unable to find healing unless someone else prays for them. One day she went into a church to pray that John's memories would be cleansed. The next time she saw him he said, "All of a sudden I feel different. Somehow I know that those rages will not come back."

They didn't. And John's leg never broke again.[1]

God Is Speaking

The first verses of Genesis tell us something else about the beginning of creation. Not only was God working, but He spoke: "Let there be light." And there was light.

Perhaps God is speaking to you and to me.

A few years ago a woman in her fifties was asked to run for president of her country. She not only had no desire to go into politics—more important, she knew it could cost her life. She is Corazon Aquino, whose husband was assassinated while he was seeking the presidency of the Philippines. A number of other individuals had been gunned down for the same "crime."

Mrs. Aquino was asked by a number of people to run for the presidency, and she prayed about it. Then she went on a special retreat, hoping to find guidance. Her prayer was very simple: "Lord, please help me to know what to do."

The answer came. Corazon got the strong conviction that she should indeed seek the presidency of her country. You probably remember those remarkable scenes when the Philippine people marched out into the streets on Corazon's behalf, interposing their frail bodies against the guns and tanks of the military dictatorship. She and the people won. A gentle Christian housewife became president of the Philippines. For several years she sought to govern her country in a truly democratic manner. The year after her landslide election, *Time* magazine featured her as Woman of the Year.

If you face a dark time, listen for the quiet voice that can guide you aright.

Light and Life Will Come

One way to move out of darkness into the warmth of God's light is simply to look up. In Psalm 34:5 we read, "They looked unto him, and were lightened."

Senator Everett Dirksen was once doing some very close reading when his eyes began to bother him. Consulting several distinguished opthalmologists, he was shocked to find that they believed he had a tumor behind his right eye. He accepted their verdict, however, and took a train to the Johns Hopkins Medical School in Baltimore to have the eye removed.

During the train ride, Dirksen, a somewhat bluff but deeply religious man, asked God about the eye situation. When he met the chief surgeon of Johns Hopkins, he said, "I have decided not to go ahead with the operation."

The surgeon couldn't believe it. He reminded the senator that the examining physicians had been unanimous in the opinion that Dirksen's eye must be removed. Dirksen replied, "I have received another opinion."

"You consulted someone else?" the surgeon asked incredulously.

"Yes. The Doctor Upstairs."

"Oh," said the surgeon. "You're one of those."

Everett Dirksen refused to have his right eye removed. Years later he said, "This is my best eye."

The Gospel of John begins in a manner remarkably similar to the Book of Genesis. "In the beginning," it says, "was the Word." That Word was Jesus: "In him was life; and the life was the light of men" (John 1:1–4). Life and light will come to you as you listen to Him.

Whatever your darkness, God is there; He is working; He has something to tell you, and He will bring light out of your darkness and healing and hope into your life.

When some dreadful tragedy happens, it is natural to ask, "Why me?" The story of Joseph in the closing chapters of the Book of Genesis offers some important clues to the mystery of pain and disappointment.

Joseph, the second youngest of a large family, was treated terribly by his older brothers. Perhaps he brought some of their anger on himself, for he kept telling them of his dreams in which they and even his father and mother bowed down to him as though he were the king. In addition, Jacob, his father, evidently treated Joseph with unwise favoritism in giving him a beautiful "coat of many colors." In any event, Joseph's brothers got rid of him by selling him into slavery in Egypt.

Years later the tables turned—as tables often do. Joseph worked his way up to one of the highest positions in Egypt. When famine devastated the Near East, his brothers heard that there was grain in Egypt and went there to buy some. Little did they realize that behind the regalia of the Egyptian official who negotiated with them was their long-lost brother.

Now the brothers were at Joseph's mercy, but he magnanimously forgave them and embraced them. Joseph knew a wonderful secret. He told his brothers, "Ye thought evil against me, but God meant it for good" (Genesis 50:20). What seems evil to us may hide God's secret plan for our good.

Indeed, "All things work together for good to them that love God" (Romans 8:28). Our loving heavenly Father is working for our benefit in everything. That is true even when things look darkest. On the wall of one business office is a poster with the message: "Please Be Patient with Me. God Isn't Finished with Me Yet." God is not only working for us, but in us and through us.

He works through us to help others. Paul wrote to the Christian believers in Corinth: "Blessed be the God and Father of our Lord Jesus Christ, the Father of mercies and God of all comfort, who comforts us in all our afflictions, so that we may be able to comfort those who are in any affliction, with the comfort with which we ourselves are comforted by God" (2 Corinthians 1:3–4 RSV). Only in our sufferings can we experience the divine comfort which we can share with others when they suffer.

Longfellow was right when he wrote, "Into each life some rain must fall." If it never rained, your lawn would wither and die. Grass needs not only sunshine but also periods of darkness, cold, and rain. Some dark days may help us grow!

The great king and psalm writer, David, had plenty of troubles. As a young shepherd, he had faced both bears and lions and protected his sheep from them. After killing Goliath, David was taken into King Saul's household. But Saul was subject to jealous rages; during one of them he picked up his spear and tried to pin David to his tent wall. After he became king, David suffered the awful blow of losing a child. When he was older, he was betrayed by his own sons who wanted to take the throne from him. But he knew his God had led him through all those dark valleys in safety. He wrote in Psalm 34:19: "Many are the afflictions of the righteous: but the LORD delivereth him out of them all."

Six Steps to the Light

1. *Move up from desperation to affirmation.* One reason so many people love David's psalms is that, while they often voice cries of desperate need, they much more often affirm the greatness and goodness and deliverance of God. See, for example, Psalms 1, 3, 8, 9, 11, 23, 34, 100, and 150.

Make these affirmations part of your life. Begin every day by affirming Psalm 118:24. Personalize it. Say, "This is the day which the LORD has made. I will rejoice and be glad in it." Throughout the day repeat, "The LORD is my shepherd; I shall not want" (Psalm 23:1). And let your last words at night be, "He gives his beloved sleep" (Psalm 127:2) or some other affirmation of God's care. What you deeply believe and strongly affirm has the power to become reality. If you want good days, affirm the power and love of God.

2. *Move up from the negative to the positive.* The Bible contains many warnings against sin and condemnations of the wicked. But it is filled even more with promises of blessings, encouragements to believe, affirmations of hope and joy, and assurances of God's unconditional love. Notice all the positive statements of this kind.

In the twenty-third Psalm, for example, David mentions enemies and death, but doesn't dwell on them. What he does emphasize is his trust that God will lead him right through the valley of the shadow of death into the sunlight of faith: "Goodness and mercy shall follow me all the days of my life: and I will dwell in the house of the LORD for ever" (verse 6).

If anyone has the right to a negative outlook, surely it must be Lena Marie Johansson of Sweden. Born with no arms, she might well be excused for giving in to pessimism and despair.

But Lena was brought up by Christian parents who learned from the Bible and positive scriptural teaching how to cope with a severely handicapped daughter. "My parents treated me like a normal person, never as a handicapped person," Marie testifies. She went to church and Sunday school—and there she acquired a strong personal faith.

Today Lena eats and works with her feet. She drives a car with special equipment. She has won swimming competitions. And she has a beautiful voice. After she sang recently at Robert Schuller's Crystal Cathedral, she was given a standing ovation. Watching her sing, one forgets that she has no arms and marvels instead at her radiant positive personality.

3. *Move up from hoping to knowing.* Don't just hope vaguely that God will bless you. Job wrote, "I know that my redeemer liveth" (Job 19:25). Paul said, "I know whom I have believed, and am persuaded that he is able to keep that which I have committed unto him" (2 Timothy 1:12). Jesus tells us, "I know my sheep, and am known of mine" (John 10:14). He knows us, and He wants us to know Him—intimately, personally, confidently, as one knows an old and trusted friend.

Dr. Lloyd Ogilvie, pastor of the First Presbyterian Church of Hollywood, once had a trustee who had money and connections—

but lacked something vital. He couldn't understand why the church should give money to people in need, particularly in other countries. One day this trustee said to Lloyd, "I confess that I don't know this Christ you keep talking about so personally." That conversation led to others, and one day the trustee committed his life to Jesus Christ. After that he took a deep interest in the church's work with people who had problems and in sending missionaries around the world. Once he remarked, "What unsettles me is those years when I decided things on my own before I knew the Lord!"

There is no substitute for knowing God personally. Give yourself to Him through Christ, do what He says, follow Him as completely as you can, and you will come to know Him as your faithful, lifelong Friend and Guide.

4. *Move up from the general to the specific.* The Bible is very specific about God. Psalm 18, for example, refers to God in very concrete terms. The psalmist calls the Lord his rock, his fortress, his deliverer, his refuge, his shelter, his hiding place, his helper, his shepherd, his king, his strong tower, his strength, and his hope. One man I know says God is his doctor, his advisor, his psychiatrist, his friend, his source of supply, and his miracle worker. How would you describe what God means to you? The more specifically you think of Him, the more He can help you.

A retired minister in Pawling, New York, has had the custom for many years of writing a letter to God every morning. "I write down the problems I am facing," he told a friend, "and eventually a solution comes. The answer, of course, is in the Bible."

Be specific in your goals and in your prayers. The less you generalize and the more you focus specifically on an objective or a need, the more you will grow spiritually.

5. *Move up from the theoretical to the personal.* One man, asked how he thought of God, admitted that his picture of the Almighty was "an oblong blur"! God is not some unknown power or impersonal "it." The Bible speaks of Him as He, Him, Thou, and You. Get to know Him as your personal Friend.

During the nineteenth century a remarkable woman named Sojourner Truth traveled widely in the cause of justice and freedom. A former slave, she was a keen thinker and an eloquent speaker. Several years ago the devotional annual *Daily Guideposts* explained one source of Sojourner Truth's power.

She often walked from place to place in order to speak. But when she was in her late seventies, some Quaker friends in Battle Creek, Michigan, loaned her their horse and buggy for easier traveling. Someone, however, discovered that Sojourner Truth could neither read nor write. How can she get anywhere without being able to read? many people wondered. When one individual got up the courage to ask Sojourner this, she explained: "When I come to a crossroads, I let the reins go slack, close my eyes, and say, 'God, You drive.' And He always takes me to a place where I have a good meeting."[2]

6. *Move up from the past to the present.* Is your faith a leftover from childhood, a relic from past years, or a present-day living faith in your greatest Friend? The Bible not only recounts what God has done in the past but also shows what He wants to do for you right now. He is "a very present help in trouble" (Psalm 46:1). He says, "Now is the accepted time; behold, now is the day of salvation" (2 Corinthians 6:2).

The twenty-third Psalm is all in the present tense! "The LORD is my shepherd . . . he leadeth me . . . thou art with me." His goodness and mercy follow us all the days of our life (Psalm 23:6)—day by day, hour by hour, moment by moment.

How to Get Up When You Are Down

When you feel "down" and depressed, it is often difficult to move up to a health-giving attitude. One way to do so is hinted at in the Gospel of Mark.

When I am not speaking somewhere I often drop in at the white-spired church near my farm, Christ Church on Quaker Hill. One Sunday while I was worshiping there, the pastor at that time, my good friend "Bern" Brunsting, spoke about this very topic. (To Bern I am indebted for the title of this section.)

Bern's message sent me back to my Bible, where I read again the story of how a sick, tired lady got a lift. The story, in Mark 1:28–31, takes place in Capernaum on the Sea of Galilee. Capernaum is still there today; I have visited it many times and walked through the ruins of its ancient synagogue.

When Jesus was in Galilee, He was worshiping in that synagogue (or one that stood there before it) when a man began making a raucous commotion. Jesus cast out the evil spirit that had obsessed the man, and peace came over him, astounding everyone. Then He and His disciples went home with Peter for a quiet meal.

But they found Peter's mother-in-law, who probably wished she could serve them, sick in bed. A fever raced through her body. When Jesus saw her, He "took her by the hand, and lifted her up," and the fever left her (verse 31). Restored to health, she served her guests a refreshing meal.

There is wondrous power in "the touch of the Master's hand." He grasped the hand of a boy with severe problems and restored him to health (Mark 9:27). He healed a leper with His touch (Mark 1:40–42). Many were healed simply by touching His robe (Mark 6:56).

And that power is available right now. Reach out to Him in faith and He will lift you up.

For a lift from the Lord, I suggest that you sit down in a quiet place and picture or visualize yourself in His presence. Close your eyes. Think of His healing power and loving touch. Picture Him coming into your home, into your room. See His loving smile. Sense His confident power. Feel His hand touching yours. Thrill to that miraculous touch. Let Him lift you back to wholeness and joy.

Nothing Need Keep You Down

The Bible is very clear about God's special love for you. You are His child, made in His image and recreated in the likeness of Jesus. You are very precious to Him. For centuries and millennia He has been reaching down and lifting those who turned to Him in trust. David described his experience of God's love in this way:

> I waited patiently for the LORD; and he inclined unto me, and heard my cry. He brought me up also out of a horrible pit, out of the miry clay, and set my feet upon a rock, and established my goings. And

he hath put a new song in my mouth, even praise unto our God: many shall see it, and fear, and shall trust in the LORD.

Psalm 40:1–3

Nothing can keep you down if you let the Lord lift you up.

The Bible is filled with records of victory over seemingly impossible odds. They might be summed up in the testimony of Paul, who said, "We are troubled on every side, yet not distressed; we are perplexed, but not in despair; persecuted, but not forsaken; cast down, but not destroyed" (2 Corinthians 4:8–9). William Barclay translates those words in this striking fashion:

> We are under pressure on every side,
> but never without a way out.
> We are at our wit's end,
> but never at our hope's end.
> We are pursued by men,
> but never abandoned by God.
> We are knocked down,
> but never knocked out.

There is a way through or over or around whatever problem looms before you. Never let a difficulty get you down. If it does, trust the good Lord to lift you to new heights.

If you are experiencing trouble or sadness:

1. Remember that God is there in the darkness with you.
2. Believe that God is working.
3. Listen to what He tells you.
4. "Trust and obey, for there's no other way to be happy in Jesus but to trust and obey."
5. Remember that all things work together for good when we love God and live as He directs.
6. Take these positive steps: Affirm God's presence, get to know Him, trust Him personally, and live in the present.
7. When you are down, let the Lord lift you up.

HAVE
A GOOD DAY
EVERY DAY

4

ne of the things my wife, Ruth, and I greatly enjoy is our school for ministers and their spouses, held twice each year. Our purpose at these four-day sessions is to share some of the techniques we have found useful in helping build faith and hope into congregations, and to show how a worship service can be an opportunity for miracles to happen. We call this phase of our work the School of Practical Christianity because we try to apply the teachings of the Bible to everyday life. We seek to show what a profound difference these teachings can make.

At one of these meetings Ruth talked with a minister's wife who seemed unusually listless and sad. The woman said she had been so depressed for years that she was unable to give any help to her husband in his work. In fact, she had become instead a great drain on his emotional resources. She had been treated by various counselors and psychiatrists with no success. She just felt miserable, she said, all the time.

"You have a choice every day," Ruth told her. "Thirty choices per month, 365 choices every year. You can choose every morning whether you will be depressed and miserable or whether you will be happy."

This was a startling new idea to this woman, and she decided to try it. About two months later she wrote that this simple practice of choice had changed her life. Every morning she made a decision to be happy for at least the next twelve hours. As a result she started enjoying all the activities of the church for the first time in years. She became an enthusiastic helper for her minister husband and finally was elected president of the women's society.

> **You have a choice every day . . . You can choose every morning whether you will be depressed and miserable or whether you will be happy.**

This experience and numerous others like it confirm my conviction that anyone can enjoy a good day every day.

This does not mean that life will be soft or easy. The Book of Proverbs reminds us, "Thou knowest not what a day may bring forth" (27:1). A few years ago Ruth and I were planning to make a winter trip to Hong Kong when I had what I thought was a great idea. "Let's cancel that trip," I told her, "and go to the Greenbriar Hotel in West Virginia instead." (*It's beautiful there,* I was thinking, *and almost as warm as Hong Kong—and a lot less expensive!*)

Ruth agreed, somewhat to my surprise, for it was she who had suggested the trip to Hong Kong. But when we got to our destination, on February 14, my brilliant idea suddenly lost its luster: The ground was covered with six inches of snow! I decided I had made a foolish mistake and started preparing to return home.

But Ruth wasn't about to let a snowfall spoil our vacation. "Norman," she said, "we're here, we can't get our money back, and it's Valentine's Day. So whether we like it or not, we're going to enjoy ourselves."

Believe it or not, we did! We found all kinds of things to do in spite of the snow. Furthermore, along with all the fun we had, I finished three chapters of a book I was writing.

Yes, disappointments and crises, even tragedies, come sooner or later to all of us. But they need not destroy our faith, nor the joy that is deeper than happiness. In this chapter I want to share some techniques that can give you a good day every day no matter what happens.

Every Day Is God's Gift

One thing the Bible emphasizes is that God gives us life in special twenty-four-hour segments. At the beginning of creation He made the days (Genesis 1:5). After each of the days of creation He "saw that it was good" (1:10, 12, ff.). When we learn to take life one day at a time and to follow scriptural principles of life and happiness, we too can look back at the end of each day, filled though it may be with pressures and problems, and thank God for a good day.

The average life contains between twenty thousand and thirty thousand days. That is a lot of days! But God gives them to us only one at a time. And His goodness and love fill every one of them (Psalms 23:6; 27:4). We can either enjoy each day and live it to the full, or we can waste it in futility and misery. The Bible was written to help us make each day wonderful.

If you take a Bible dictionary or concordance and look up some of the references to *day, today, tomorrow, yesterday, morning,* and *new,* you will find that the Bible speaks often about the twenty-four-hour principle. For example, the twenty-third Psalm concludes, "Surely goodness and mercy shall follow me *all the days of my life.*" The Lord's Prayer reminds us to ask *this day* for *our daily bread* (emphasis mine).

The Bible is a present-tense book. Although it does tell us about the past and the future, it concentrates on *today.* "The LORD *is* my shepherd . . . He *leadeth* me [right now] . . . He *restoreth* my soul" (Psalm 23:1–3). "The earth *is* the LORD'S" (Psalm 24:1). "The LORD *is* my light" (Psalm 27:1, emphasis mine).

Our heavenly Father wants us to "show forth from day to day his salvation" (1 Chronicles 16:23). On the Israelites' journey through the wilderness toward the Promised Land, God sent them a white, delicious food that made them ask "Man-nuh?" ("What is it?") So it was called manna. Every morning it fell like snow and provided satisfying food for the day. Some of the people tried to gather enough for the next day or two, but it always spoiled if kept beyond the day it was gathered (Exodus 16:11–20). God seems to have been making it clear that He wants us to live one day at a time.

This does not mean that planning for the future is not important. Jesus told parables about the foolishness of not looking ahead.

One was the story of the man who started to build a tower but had to leave it unfinished because he did not initially count the cost (Luke 14:28–30).

But our Savior also said, "Take no thought for the morrow" (Matthew 6:34). This could be better translated, "Take no anxious thought about tomorrow" or "Do not worry about the future." It is not thinking but worrying that ruins life. We live to the fullest by living one day at a time.

Each day is special from God, delivered to us as His choice present, hand-wrapped for our benefit and enjoyment. If we take each day as His gift, it will be the blessing He intends for us.

One of my college classmates became an unusually successful salesman. Once, at dinner in his Chicago apartment, we got on the subject of having a great day. "Come here," he said, and he pointed to a card fastened to his bathroom mirror. On it I read:

> Want a great day?
> Believe a great day.
> Think a great day.
> Pray a great day.
> Deserve a great day.
> Take God with you for a great day.
> Get going and make it a great day.

Now, with thanks to my classmate, Judson Sayre, I want to elaborate on some of those points as we follow, more or less, his formula for a great day.

Begin Each Day with God

Psychologists say that the whole day is conditioned by two five-minute periods: The five minutes before we go to sleep at night and the first five minutes when we awake. "It is a good thing," wrote the psalmist (Psalm 92:1–2), "to give thanks unto the LORD, and to sing praises unto thy name, O most High, to show forth thy loving-kindness in the morning, and thy faithfulness every night."

Follow that ancient wisdom for a great day. When you wake up, give thanks to God for life and health and strength, and for all His blessings in your life. And when you go to bed, thank Him for His faithful guidance and loving mercies through the day.

Dr. Raj K. Chopra is a man who learned the hard way how to make the most of each day. Born in India, at the age of ten he lost his father to cancer. A few months later he witnessed the fighting between Moslems and Hindus that resulted in the murder of his mother's parents and the slaughter of thousands of natives.

In the turmoil Raj hid with his mother and siblings until they were taken to a refugee camp. There he started raising goats to provide food for his family. He would probably be one of India's hapless millions today if he had not had a devout grandmother.

After searching for months, Raj's paternal grandmother found the family. She told the boy: "You have a greater purpose in life, Raj, than tending goats. You are somebody. You are going to get an education. God has a special plan for you."

Through his grandmother's positively oriented influence Raj Chopra acquired a deep faith and a life purpose. He decided God wanted him to serve Him in education—and set himself the goal of becoming a superintendent of schools in America.

Reaching the goal was not easy. But he worked until he earned a Ph.D. and was teaching in America. Then he accepted the job of superintendent of schools in one of the worst school systems in the United States. After three years he made it one of the nation's best.

Dr. Chopra has written a book entitled *Making a Bad Situation Good*, in which he describes the "power principles" that guided his success. One of them is a daily spiritual warm-up similar to that of an athlete who knows he has to prepare before a game.

The first part of this daily warm-up is a "count your blessings exercise." Dr. Chopra suggests:

> Begin by saying three good things about yourself. ("You're looking good today, [*your name*].") . . . Next, list three good things about the place in which you live . . . and last, name aloud three of your blessings . . .
>
> Such a mental pep talk sets the tone for the day ahead. And the enthusiasm is carried one step further by daily affirming each family member's importance through hugs and a brief sharing time at the breakfast table . . . By accepting every day with a sense of grateful-

ness and thanksgiving, and by mentally warming up, our spirits are uplifted, and we are ready to accept the best in any situation.[1]

My friend George Shinn is the youngest person who ever received the Horatio Alger Award, which goes annually to someone who started poor and achieved something remarkable. George comes from a very poor family in North Carolina. Earning his tuition in business college by working as a janitor, George was able to invest enough of his savings to become one of the school's owners. But soon afterward his outstanding business career nearly crashed. Now he was so deeply in debt that one of his associates told him, "You don't have a prayer."

Then George Shinn realized that if he didn't have anything else, he did have a prayer! He laid the whole situation before God. He asked Him to be his Partner. George is now one of the finest businessmen in the South. The morning after he turned his life and his business over to God, he felt so exhilarated that his first words on awaking were "Good morning, Lord!"

Plan a Good Day

Make today and every day a great day by planning to make it great. Good things seldom happen unless we think and work to make them happen.

Learn how to trust the Lord for His guidance in every decision. Some years ago a new employee at the Peale Center for Christian Living moved to an area where each house had its own well. Soon after moving, Don and his wife, Jeanne, woke up to find they had no water.

They checked their well and plumbing to no avail. When a neighbor said the fault was probably loss of pressure in their water tank, they emptied the tank and refilled it, but there was still no water. Then they called in the contractor who had dug the well, and he too was baffled.

That morning Jeanne followed her usual custom of beginning the day with prayer and reading the Bible. Soon afterward an idea came to her and she passed it on to the contractor. "Do you think," she asked him, "that there might be a connection between our loss of water and the fact that we just had a new telephone installed the other day?"

That led to the solution. The contractor discovered that the telephone worker in grounding a line had inadvertently split a wire from the pump. A simple solution—but it came as solutions so often do, when someone stopped to meditate and listen for God's guidance.

Each morning ask God what He wants you to do today. Is there someone you can help with a special word of greeting or encouragement or an act of Christian love? Does the Lord want you to do something new today?

Make each day a good day by affirming a good day. Say, "This is the day the LORD has made: I will rejoice and be glad in it." (Personalize this from Psalm 118:24.) Picture a good day. Expect it to be the best possible day, and it will be.

John Oxenham wrote:

> Not for one single day
> Can I discern my way,
>   But this I surely know—
> Who gives the day
> Will show the way,
>   So I securely go.[2]

What are the most important things you want to do today? Jot them down and plan how you will accomplish them. Trust God for this. Then, with His almighty help, make them happen.

Enjoy a Good Day

Intentionally savor the good things every day brings. Enjoy the morning light. Thank God for the smell of coffee, the taste of juice or eggs or bacon or oatmeal or whatever you have for breakfast. Enjoy your family, friends, and other people you meet through the day.

God wants you to enjoy many good days. "For he that would love life and see good days, let him keep his tongue from evil and his lips from speaking guile; let him turn away from evil and do right; let him seek peace and pursue it" (1 Peter 3:10–11 RSV). To make your day bright, work at it. Do what is right and don't be negative about anyone or anything. The straighter you live and the more positively you speak, the better and happier and greater each day will become.

Let Jesus Christ help you enjoy life more. A man wrote me:

> One day after the birth of my son and daughter, I began feeling I had no future. That's an awful feeling.
>
> I bought a book of yours and began reading. The book showed me a Jesus I had never known, a Jesus willing to help me. I began to pray, not only for myself, but for other people as well. I began to feel confidence and peace for the first time in months.

Of course, as long as we are on earth, life is bound to be filled with things that could be upsetting. But they need not disturb your inner peace. Remember our Lord's promise: "In this world you will have trouble. But take heart! I have overcome the world" (John 16:33 NIV).

A Day in the Life of Jesus

If you want to watch the divine Master meeting the most difficult stresses and interruptions, read the fifth chapter of the Gospel of Mark. After sailing across the Sea of Galilee with His disciples, Jesus first healed a severely deranged man. Then, going in the disciples' boat to another shore of the Sea of Galilee, Jesus was about to speak to a great number of people when a Jewish official named Jairus rushed up to Him and begged Him to heal his little daughter. Jesus graciously went with the man, but on the way He met still another interruption. A woman who had been hemorrhaging for twelve years quietly touched His robe. She was immediately healed. Feeling the divine healing power flow out of Him, Jesus asked who had touched Him. The woman was almost too frightened to speak, but Jesus told her to go in peace and be whole.

Immediately another interruption came as Jesus resumed His journey to heal Jairus' daughter. Messengers ran up saying the little girl was dead. The Lord's response was, "Be not afraid, only believe" (Mark 5:36). Then He went into the house of death and took the little girl's hand and life flowed back into her.

With all these problems and interruptions surrounding Jesus, He remained Master of each situation. Taking each difficulty as it came, He responded to it cooly and victoriously. And so can we, if we refuse to let anything throw us. Instead, we can call upon Him for whatever help we need in meeting and mastering each problem. Remember: "Be not afraid, only believe."

When You Make Mistakes

You will not be able to enjoy a good day if you make too many foolish mistakes. An old hymn reminds me, "Prone to wander, Lord, I feel it." We all make many errors! Now, the opposite of error is truth. Jesus tells us, "I am the way, the truth, and the life" (John 14:6). If you take Him as your Savior and Guide, follow Him and trust Him, you will be filled with life and truth. And truth pushes out error. The more of Him and His truth you possess, the more good days you will have.

If you are an average human being, something may occur soon to make you angry. The Bible tells us, "Be angry, and sin not: let not the sun go down upon your wrath" (Ephesians 4:26). We should be angry at cruelty or cheating or injustice or any kind of evil. But we don't need to let the events of the day destroy our night's rest or the next day's joy. What the Bible recommends is: (1) Be sure our anger, if we have any, is fundamentally righteous anger; (2) refuse to give in to ordinary sinful anger; and (3) end the anger at nightfall. Before the day ends make peace with whoever disturbed you if that is possible. Think your way toward a constructive solution of whatever angered you. Do what you can to right what is wrong. And then leave the rest with God and go to sleep.

Make God a Vital Part of Your Day

If you want the best possible day, make your Father and Lord a vital part of it. Refuse to even think of doing or saying anything mean or shady. Keep God in your thoughts.

Dr. Frank Laubach taught millions of people in dozens of countries to read and write through three things. One was his unique literacy chart, which converted the alphabet into visual symbols and helped illiterates to read with amazing rapidity. The second was his love for people. He used to sit down with an illiterate Asian or African, put his arm around the person, and love him or her into the ability to read.

The third secret of Frank Laubach's power was his constant walk with God. He invented a "Game with Minutes" in which he kept track of how often he thought of God during each hour. As he was able to set his mind more and more on the Lord, his success as a world evangelist through literacy grew greater and greater.

Frank Laubach also talked constantly with God. On a plane or bus he liked to "shoot prayers" at strangers; often they would turn and smile at him, so evidently the prayer did something warm and wonderful for that individual.

I do the same thing myself, and it actually does work! In the club car of a train, years ago, a man across from me was obviously very drunk. His tongue was loosened and he was saying things I was certain were confidential. I shot prayers at him that he would stop talking. He looked directly at me and made a gesture of agreement with his hand.

Soon he got up and, with a gesture of good night, left the car. The next morning, sober, he remembered and thanked me for stopping him. The sequel is that this businessman has been "dry" for twenty years.

The great King David communicated with God through his psalms. When David felt low, he told God about it. When he was exuberant, he thanked and praised Him.

Jesus was constantly in touch with His heavenly Father. He said repeatedly that what He did resulted from understanding what His Father wanted and obeying His words (John 6:38; 8:29).

End the Day with God

There is a story that the great Bishop Quayle was very worried about a severe problem. That night as he lay awake tossing the problem back and forth in his mind, he felt he heard God say, "Quayle, you go to sleep and let Me worry about it."

When you undress at night, undress your mind too. Your mental pockets fill each day with bits and scraps of things that you do not need to carry forever with you. At bedtime review the things of the day and in your imagination drop into the wastebasket everything that is not worth preserving. Throw out your worries, your fears, and your memories of anything spiteful, critical, unjust, unloving, or negative.

Then, before you go to sleep, fill your mind with thoughts of goodness and love and faith and hope, thoughts of God and Jesus. As these thoughts permeate your mind and heart, they will restore your soul while you sleep.

One thing that destroys happiness is to let the problems and worries of the day come back into our minds as we mentally relax. God sends darkness every day so we can blot out such negative thoughts. If they crowd into your mind at night, try mentally projecting each one onto a giant blackboard. Then picture it being erased. Now fill the screen of your imagination with pictures of serenity and faith, of goodness and love.

A Sure Way to a Happy Day

Remember that you can only live one day at a time. Yesterday is a memory. Tomorrow is a hope. The only reality is right now. Make this minute a good one, fill it with love and trust and good deeds; continue this all day and every day, and your life will be full of happiness.

Helen Steiner of Lorain, Ohio, was only sixteen when her father died in the flu epidemic that followed World War I. Graduating that year from high school, she went to work to help her mother and younger sister. Helen soon became director of public relations for the Ohio Public Service Company and became one of the few woman speakers of the time. I like some of her lecture topics: "Blue Eyes or Gray Matter?" and "Living and Working Enthusiastically."

Helen caught the eye of a handsome young banker named Franklin Rice and married him just before the Great Depression. Caught up in the euphoria of the times, he had put everything he could borrow into the stock market when it crashed and took everything he owned. One morning Helen woke up to find Franklin gone, leaving her only a suicide note: *I just can't go down and become a bum—I have to go out with the bands playing.*

Out of that experience Helen Steiner Rice began writing the verses that have helped make the Christian faith a practical reality in the lives of thousands of her readers. Here is her philosophy of living, entitled "A Sure Way to a Happy Day":

> Happiness is something we create in our mind.
>   It's not something you search for and so seldom find—
> It's just waking up and beginning the day
>   By counting our blessings and kneeling to pray—
> It's giving up thoughts that breed discontent
>   and accepting what comes as a "gift heaven-sent"—
> It's giving up wishing for things we have not
>   And making the best of whatever we've got—
> It's knowing that life is determined for us,
>   And pursuing our tasks—without fret, fume or fuss—
> For it's by completing what God gives us to do
>   that we find real contentment
>   and happiness too.[3]

Every day think a good day, plan a good day, pray a good day, and make it a good day! And you will be able to say with the psalmist, "Every day will I bless thee" (Psalm 145:2).

For a good day every day:

1. Accept each day as God's special new gift.
2. Every morning ask Him to bless your day.
3. Start the day with a spiritual warm-up. Count your blessings and believe this will be one of your best days.
4. Think a good day. We generally get what we expect.
5. Plan a good day. Picture in detail twenty-four satisfying hours.
6. Work your plan.
7. Enjoy a good day. Don't let anything that happens keep you from making the best of this day.
8. Make God and doing good a vital part of your day.
9. End your day with thanksgiving for the day behind you, and for the night and the morrow before you.

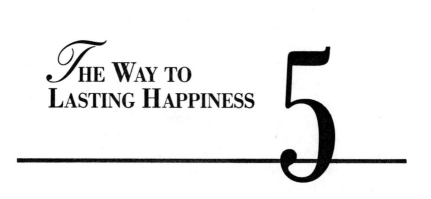

THE WAY TO LASTING HAPPINESS

ears ago that great Scottish entertainer, Harry Lauder, sang some words that still ring in the memories of some of us. As I remember, one song went like this:

Oh, it's nice to get up in the morning
  when the sun begins to shine,
At four or five or six o'clock
  In the good old summertime.

But when the snow is blowing
  And it's murky overhead,
Oh, it's nice to get up in the morning—
  But it's nicer to stay in bed!

Unfortunately, the emotional state of many of us often fluctuates with the weather, or goes up or down for no logical reason. But I am convinced that the Lord wants all of us to enter into a state of happiness deeper than mere feelings—an underlying joyful outlook that goes on and on, from good to better, to the best time of your life.

Robert Louis Stevenson rightly said, "To miss the joy is to miss all." That is true in many ways. Joy seems to affect the quality of the blood that flows through our veins, enhancing the quality of the red blood cells and even improving the circulation. While depressed spirits can lead to anemia and other ills, happiness and serenity often result in better blood pressure and better health in general.

Dr. E. Stanley Jones once told of an experiment some hospital personnel did with a dog. The little dog was a sort of mascot befriended by the staff; it wagged its tail each time one of the doctors or nurses spoke to it. An incision was made into a bone in the dog's leg, revealing a healthy pink condition.

Orders were then given for no one to speak to the dog. The small animal became miserable, feeling rejected. After a few days another incision was made, and this time the interior of the bone was brown, dry, and unhealthy looking. Thereupon orders were given to greet and pet the little dog as before. When a third incision was made, once more the bone tissue was pink and healthy. The Bible describes this situation quite literally in Proverbs 17:22: "A merry heart doeth good like a medicine: but a broken spirit drieth the bones."

I once knew a man who taught hundreds of people how to be continually happy. Earlier in his life, however, he had been so miserable that he drank some poison, trying to kill himself. By some miraculous intervention the poison only burned his lips. When he recovered—having never expected to see the dawn—his first thought was a negative one: *I can't even kill myself.* But then a different thought arose: *Perhaps God has spared me for a purpose.*

In that moment it was given to Jeb, as I shall call him, that his purpose was to make other humans happy. Everywhere he went for the next thirty years Jeb left a trail of sunshine and smiles. He handed people he met a business card that had printed on it the words:

The Way to Happiness

Keep your heart free from hate, your mind free from worry.
Live simply; expect little; give much;
fill your life with love; scatter sunshine.
Forget self.
Think of others, and do as you would be done by.
Try it for a week—you will be surprised.

Jeb became one of the happiest men I ever knew. He died triumphantly, and one of the last things he said was, "If ye know these things, happy are ye if ye do them" (John 13:17). If you will copy those words and learn them by heart, you will find they are a key to lasting happiness.

What are the things Jesus wants us to do to be happy? We know from his life and teachings: to develop faith, honor, humility, goodness, kindness, and generosity. Most of us know what the Lord wants us to do; and if we really do it, we enter more and more fully into the kind of happiness that lasts.

The Happiness Book

Probably a lot of people do not think of happiness in connection with the Bible. Bibles used to be bound in black, and often the preacher or priest wore a black robe. Even festivities and merrymaking were denounced in certain religious circles.

But basically the Bible is a book not of severity and gloom but of joy, even laughter. With what joy the Lord God must have created the world with all its exotic flowers, colorful birds, and strange creatures of the land and sea! The star-sprinkled sky, sunrises, sunsets, spring days, and the glory of autumn are all the handiwork of a joyful Creator.

And His Word is a book of joy. Leah exulted, "Happy am I" when her son was born (Genesis 30:13). The Virgin Mary rejoiced at the thought of giving birth to Jesus: "My soul doth magnify the Lord, and my spirit hath rejoiced in God my Savior" (Luke 1:46–47). The angel who announced Christ's birth said, "I bring you good tidings of great joy" (Luke 2:10).

God was so eager for His people to enjoy Him that He warned of disaster if they did not serve Him "with joyfulness, and with gladness of heart" (Deuteronomy 2:47–48). The Bible word "blessed" is a word of joy; John Wesley translated "blessed" in the Beatitudes (Matthew 5:3–12) as "happy." And rightly so, for blessedness is, as someone has said, "happiness with its roots in eternity." So the "Be-Attitudes," as my friend Robert Schuller calls the Beatitudes, reveal the way to joyous living.

Jesus continually sounded the note of joy in His life and teachings. When the good shepherd left his ninety-nine sheep to look for the one lost lamb and found it, he carried it home on his shoulders "rejoicing." The woman who searched her house for a lost coin until she found it called to her friends, "Rejoice with me." Just so, said Jesus, "joy shall be in heaven" when one lost person finds the Father (Luke 15:3–10). The kingdom of heaven is like a treasure someone finds, "and for joy thereof goeth and selleth all that he hath" (Matthew 13:44).

The fruit of the Spirit begins with love, joy, and peace (Galatians 5:22). The joy of the Lord is our strength (Nehemiah 8:10). God's desire for us is that we may be filled with all joy and peace in believing (Romans 15:13).

All through the Bible the love between God and his people is pictured as the love of a man for his bride, and the most beautiful portrait of how it will end depicts a wedding and a happy marriage.

In Scripture, giving is not a grim duty but a joyful opportunity. Paul tells us, "God loveth a cheerful giver" (2 Corinthians 9:7). The word Paul actually used for cheerful, *hilarion*, could well be translated "hilarious." God wants exuberant happiness in all we do!

Even trouble is transmuted, through the golden touch of faith, into happiness. "Count it all joy, my brothers," James writes in the Bible, "when you meet various trials, for you know that the testing of your faith produces steadfastness. And let steadfastness have its full effect, that you may be perfect and complete, lacking in nothing" (James 1:2–4 RSV). In other words, face your troubles with joyous faith in the Lord who makes us victorious over our problems, and your character will become whole and mature and continually radiant.

My friend Sam Shoemaker once said, "The surest mark of a Christian is not faith, or even love, but joy."

As Father Higenio Alas was celebrating a mass in Costa Rica, he conducted a dialogue with members of his congregation. When he asked a seven-year-old girl, "Who is God?" everyone was surprised by her answer: "God is joy."

"What about Jesus on the cross?" asked Father Higenio.

"Oh, yes," said the child. "He had perfect joy then, because at that moment He was giving everything He was and had to those He loved. He had to be very happy at that moment."

A neighbor tells me that one Sunday a woman sitting next to him in Marble Collegiate Church confided, "We laugh a lot here. We never laughed in church before Dr. Peale came." I was glad to hear this observation, for a merry heart indeed does good like a medicine.

How to Be Happy

The German philosopher Goethe said there are nine keys to contentment:

1. Health enough to make work a pleasure.
2. Money enough to support your needs.
3. Strength enough to battle your difficulties and overcome them.
4. Grace enough to confess your sins and forsake them.
5. Patience enough to work until some good is accomplished.
6 Charity enough to see some good in your neighbors.
7. Love enough to move you to be useful and helpful to others.
8. Faith enough to make real the things of God.
9. Hope enough to remove all anxious fears concerning the future.

Notice how practical Goethe's keys are. Notice also how spiritually motivated most of them are. But how do we acquire enough strength, grace, patience, love, and so on to find contentment? The Bible gives us many important clues to finding abiding happiness. Here are a few:

Happy is that people, whose God is the Lord (Psalm 144:15).
Happy is the man that findeth wisdom (Proverbs 3:13).
He that hath mercy on the poor, happy is he (Proverbs 14:21).
Whoso trusteth in the Lord, happy is he (Proverbs 16:20).
Blessed [happy] are the poor in spirit [humble] (Matthew 5:3).
These things have I spoken unto you, that my joy might remain in you and that your joy might be full (John 15:11).

The kingdom of God is . . . righteousness, and peace, and joy in the
   Holy Ghost (Romans 14:17).
Happy is he that condemneth not himself (Romans 14:22).
We count them happy which endure (James 5:11).

Begin putting these verses into practice in your daily life, and
you will be blessed beyond measure.

Find Joy through Victorious Tranquillity

One necessity for a life of happiness is to have a quiet, calm, un-
nervous mental attitude. This is easier said than done, but if you
will reject worry thoughts and try to look at everything from the
perspective of serene tranquillity, you will find the joy of the Lord
flooding your soul.

My wife, Ruth, tells me she found a living illustration of this when
she spoke at a convention of farmers in North Dakota. In her words:

"At a lunch that day I sat across from a man who looked serene
but seemed shy. To draw him out, I asked an obvious question: 'How
are the crops?' His face reddened a little as he answered, 'They ain't
very good.'

"When I asked why, this farmer said, 'We had a big dust storm
that ruined seventy-five percent of our crops. Then we had a swarm
of grasshoppers that ate up near everything else. I was lucky, I saved
five percent of my crop. But my brother, on the farm next to me,
lost everything he had. I try to help him out a little.'

"I said, 'My! That is dreadful! You must be terribly worried and
upset.' To which he replied, 'No, Ma'am, I ain't upset. You see, there
is nothing I can do about it, so I just aim to forget it. Jesus helps
me see that life is full of this and that. I hope to do better next time.'"

With faith and an attitude like that, you can keep free from tension and have a happier outlook.

What Destroys Happiness?

Another key to lasting happiness is avoiding what brings unhap-
piness. Many things do this, but most boil down to one thing: sin.
Doing what is wrong in any way simply takes the joy out of life.
Every one of us knows how true this is.

Psalm 51 is a wonderful description of the effects of sin and the blessing of forgiveness. The subtitle says this is a psalm of David when the prophet Nathan faced him about his sin with Bathsheba. The story is in the eleventh chapter of 2 Samuel.

One hot summer night, we can imagine, King David could not sleep. He was pacing the roof of his palace when something caught his eye. From his rooftop he could see a woman bathing. It was the beautiful Bathsheba, the wife of one of his best soldiers.

David knew Bathsheba's husband Uriah was away on the battle-front. He sent a message for Bathsheba to come to the palace. When the king learned that a pregnancy had resulted, he plotted to cover up what had happened. He called Uriah home and bade him visit his wife. But good soldier Uriah vowed that he would not go near her until his wartime tour of duty was over.

That ploy failing, David played another card. He sent word for Uriah to be put at the front of the battle line during the next conflict—and then to pull back, leaving him alone under enemy fire. The wicked scheme worked only too well. Uriah was killed, ostensibly in the line of duty.

So to adultery David added the sin of murder, virtually in cold blood. But there was a man of God who dared to confront the king! The prophet Nathan was brave enough to tell his king, who could have snuffed out his life too, what was right in God's sight. And King David was man enough to admit his double sin. He knew that salvation means joy, and he had strayed from his Lord and lost the joy. And because at the bottom of his heart he loved God more than anything else, he wanted that joy back.

David acknowledged his sin and begged for cleansing (Psalm 51:1–3). He prayed, "Restore unto me the joy of thy salvation" (verse 12). He knew that when he was forgiven and restored, his happiness would return (verses 8, 14, 15).

Whatever you do, if you want to be happy, avoid sin. And if you do fail, confess it and the Lord will restore to you, too, the joy of salvation.

Bring Happiness to Others

Down in South Carolina is one of the happiest individuals I know of. John Fling, of Columbia, makes a habit of giving whatever he can to anyone in need. During the past few years he has given away five cars! "Doing for other people gives me a satisfied mind," he says.

One winter John gave the socks he was wearing to a man with none. He is a big brother to hundreds of men, women, and children. And John has a special concern for the blind: He invented a unique jogging wheel that enables his unsighted friends to get aerobic exercise with him. He regularly provides several hundred children with clothing, food, candy, and toys.

Is John Fling rich? "I've always been poor and always will be," he says. But in terms of good health and happiness, he is one of the richest men in the world.

An article about John Fling in *Parade* magazine shows him surrounded by a group of poor children. But you would never know they are poor, their faces are so filled with joy. And the most joyous face of all is that of the man in the center.

Yes, real living is giving. "Those who bring sunshine to the lives of others," said the great writer James Barrie, "cannot keep it from themselves."

Let's return to the Epistle of James. Not only does James show us how to find joy even in our troubles, he also points the way to the abiding joy of the Lord. It is what real religion is about:

> Pure religion and undefiled before God and the Father is this, to visit the fatherless and widows in their affliction, and to keep himself unspotted from the world.
>
> James 1:27

Genuine religion, then—and a profound way to happiness—is helping those in need and keeping so deeply in tune with God's purposes that the false values of the world are unable to stain or defile us.

The Lord's Example for Us

Did anyone ever have a more lasting, deep-down spirit of joy and happiness than our Lord Jesus? Children loved Him, fishermen loved Him, businesspeople loved Him, poor people and sick people and even the worst sinners loved and followed Him. He was Love and Peace and Joy made visible. And He was always helping someone.

How do you help people? It is not always easy, but the Bible shows how Jesus did it (Mark 6:34–44). Think of these suggestions for helping someone effectively:

1. *Be aware of the need.* Jesus' heart went out to the people who followed Him, and His disciples empathized with their hunger (verses 34–36). To find happiness through helping someone else, it is important to find out what the real need is and then try to fill it.

2. *Bring the problem to Jesus.* The disciples had no idea how to help this crowd of five thousand people. What a problem! But absolutely no problem is too big for God. "Take your burden to the Lord," in the words of an old hymn, "and leave it there." So the disciples did the best thing anyone can do. They simply told Jesus about the need they saw.

3. *Do what you can.* Trust does not mean inaction. To believe in Christ and to pray may mean very definite action. The Lord may tell us exactly what to do, and this may be something we do not want to hear. Jesus told the disciples, in effect, "*You* feed them" (verse 37).

What a command! No wonder the disciples responded, almost sarcastically, "Shall we look for two hundred dollars to go buy food for this mob?" They saw no way to feed the crowd, but they could begin with what they had.

4. *Take inventory.* Jesus told the disciples to see how much food was available (verse 38). The result probably seemed almost laughable. Here were five thousand hungry people, and the disciples located five loaves of bread (probably each about the size of a pita) and two little fish! But there is an old proverb, "Little is much when God is in it."

From John's telling of this event, we know that this food was probably a little boy's lunch (John 6:1–14). That boy must have given all he had to Jesus. Out of his faith and love grew one of the greatest miracles. But it all began when the disciples looked around to see what they had.

5. *Think and organize.* When you have a problem, don't be cowed by it. Think about it—calmly, objectively, trusting in God to help you solve it. And organize what you can do. Jesus had the people sit down in groups of fifty or a hundred on the grass (Mark

6:39–40). Perhaps this helped prevent a riot. You can imagine what five thousand hungry people might do if they began stampeding to get food! Seating them first would help prevent such a tragedy.

6. *Thank God for what you have.* When Jesus looked up to heaven and blessed that little lunch (verse 41), He must have thanked God not only for the food but also for the miracle that He was about to perform. The spirit of thankfulness is part of the complex of faith and dedication that helps set the stage for miracles.

And a miracle happened. As the food was divided among the people, "they did all eat, and were filled" (verse 42). Everyone was satisfied. In fact, there were twelve baskets of leftovers (verse 43).

These are some of God's principles of true happiness. As you put them into practice in your own life, you will find blessings "pressed down and running over"—abundant and satisfying (Luke 6:38).

> **What determines happiness is the state of the mind.**

Accept the Gift of Joy

God promises, "Ye shall go out with joy, and be led forth with peace . . . With joy shall ye draw water out of the wells of salvation" (Isaiah 55:12; 12:3). The great Russian novelist Tolstoy said that when he found God, delicious waves of life surged through his being. He enjoyed life in a totally new way. And this joy comes to all of us as we open our lives to our Lord and actualize His gift of joy.

One thing I have noticed about genuinely happy people is this: It isn't how much they have or who they are that makes them joyful. What determines happiness is the state of the mind.

One of the happiest women in the Northeast was a schoolteacher. "Aunt Em," as many of her friends and relatives called her, never made a lot of money, but she immeasurably enriched the lives and enhanced the health and happiness of everyone who knew her. Part of her philosophy of living is summed up in this plaque she gave to one of my associates and his family:

> Thank God for dirty dishes!
> They have a tale to tell;
> While others may go hungry,
> We're eating very well.
>
> With home and health and happiness
> I shouldn't want to fuss;
> For by the stack of evidence
> God's been good to us.

Very simple words but a positive philosophy that can work wonders.

All of us need to do a job on our thoughts. If the mind is filled with grudges, if it is bogged down with hate or selfishness or impurity or dishonesty, the clear light of joy cannot filter through. Fill your mind and heart instead with God's words, search for the good in those you meet, get rid of impurity and negativity. Ask forgiveness for your errors and replace them with the great truths of the Bible, the words of Jesus, and the great affirmations in the Psalms and Proverbs and Epistles. Then simply accept God's gift of joy as you would accept a present from a friend. Take joy, believe joy, live joy. You will become profoundly happy.

The Seven-Day Mental Diet

Ruth and I once knew a man whom you might describe as one of our "miserable" friends. He seemed to have the ability to take the joy out of everyone around him and make them miserable, too. He was a happiness extractor and misery creator. But years later he became one of the kindest, happiest people I ever knew. He once told me why: "I went on a seven-day mental diet."

Our friend explained that someone had given him a little pamphlet by Emmet Fox, a student of Scripture whose books have helped a great many people. In this pamphlet was the seven-day diet. The idea is this: Resolve that for exactly one week you will watch every word as a cat watches a mouse. For those seven days refuse to say one mean or dishonest or depressing thing, no matter what thoughts enter your head.

Of course that is a big order. Our friend said, "I tried it one day and failed. I tried it again and went two whole days before I slipped and said something negative. I tried again and failed.

"I realized I had to change inwardly," he went on. "So I asked God to help me. Then, for one whole week, I succeeded. Being worn out with all that effort, I thought I would ease off. But, you know, I couldn't do that, for now I was changed. I had risen to a higher level. At first I felt a bit dizzy up there, but I have discovered I can live on that higher level. Now I am thinking positively and saying only positive things all the time. And life has become altogether different."

Such a seven-day program of eliminating the negative and programming mind and heart for the positive will bring anyone a similar rise to the heights of happiness.

Meet the Lord of Joy

I knew a newspaperman who was hostile to Christ and Christian things. He said he was "a modern pagan" through and through. He had taken part in all kinds of questionable activities in his search for happiness.

The strange thing was that this man's naturally happy spirit soured as he continued deeper on the path of self-indulgence. Describing it later, he said, "All the fun went out of my life."

Then he met Jesus. Surrendering his life to Him, he experienced such a joyful change in his outlook that it could best be described in these words from the New Testament: "Therefore if any man be in Christ, he is a new creature: old things are passed away; behold, all things are become new" (2 Corinthians 5:17).

One of his friends said when he heard this man had become a follower of Christ: "Life must be gloomy now."

"Oh, no," he answered. "Quite the opposite! I've been laughing ever since I met Him."

After C.S. Lewis became a Christian, he wrote about his experience in a book fittingly entitled *Surprised by Joy.* He once said, "Joy is the serious business of heaven."[1] The Bible reminds us that

Jesus "for the joy that was set before him endured the cross" (Hebrews 12:2).

For the fullest possible happiness, give yourself completely to this Master of Joy. Trust your whole life to Him. Read His words, follow His ways, talk to Him, and He will irradiate your personality with "joy unspeakable and full of glory" (1 Peter 1:8).

To enjoy life to the fullest:

1. Live for a great purpose.
2. Read the passages of joy in the Bible.
3. Practice victorious tranquillity.
4. Avoid the things that destroy happiness.
5. Bring happiness to others; it will rub off on you.
6. Accept God's gift of joy and demonstrate it in your life.
7. Try the seven-day mental diet, refusing to say anything negative for one week.
8. Walk with the Lord of joy and live in His Spirit.

THREE KEYS TO PERSONAL FREEDOM 6

*P*ositive thinking and positive living mean basically living as the Bible tells us, with faith and hope and love and joy. But most of us recognize that we have a long way to go to live that way consistently.

Consider Jesus' words, "Be ye therefore perfect, even as your Father in heaven is perfect" (Matthew 5:48). One thing that helps explain this verse is that the New Testament word for *perfect* may also be translated *complete* or *mature*. God wants us to grow up! Jesus once explained that our spiritual growth is something like the growth of a grapevine. We are attached to Jesus as branches to a vine trunk, and God sometimes has to prune the limbs of our lives so we can grow enough to bear more fruit (John 15:1–5).

All of us strive for perfection in our daily lives. When you are shopping, are you satisfied with a dented can of vegetables or a newspaper with part of a page torn off? Is it okay with you to have a radio or television set that only works part of the time, or a car that won't start in bad weather? Would you want to find a little dirt or a few pieces of glass in your food now and then?

Of course not! Neither is our heavenly Father satisfied when we fail to make progress spiritually. He wants to help us grow toward perfection.

Now let's return to Matthew 5:48. I like the way the New English Bible translates this: "There must be no limit to your goodness, as your heavenly Father's goodness knows no bounds."

We advance toward that goal through our Lord Jesus Christ. Colossians 3:4 tells us that He is our life. It is possible to go through life half-dead, not really living. Christ opens our eyes and ears and heart to all that is lastingly worthwhile and enjoyable. *He is our life.* He puts a sparkle in the eye, a song in the heart, a bounce in the step. No wonder He said, "I am the way, the truth, and the life" (John 14:6).

But to benefit from His life we have to walk His way. Becoming a Christian is not the end of our problems but the beginning of victory over them. And the result is joy unspeakable.

A young woman came to our Pawling offices a few years ago with unbelievable problems. She had not only deserted her husband and children, she had even become trapped in drugs. At one point she attempted suicide by overdosing.

Two of our counselors talked with this woman at different times and helped her turn to God. Gradually she got control of herself. After moving to another state, she sent us several letters of appreciation for the change in her life. In one letter she wrote, "Now every day is Christmas!"

That is abundant living. But some who read these words may approach each morning with dread. Some of you, I surmise, are splendidly successful in life, yet some may feel like failures. Some may have habits such as overeating or constant worrying that you cannot control. Some probably have children or grandchildren or friends who have problems with drugs or alcohol.

Whatever your situation, I believe you can reach a more satisfying level of living with these suggestions. And you may wish to share them with someone who needs help to be freed from a debilitating habit.

The Importance of Facing Life Honestly

The Bible has much to say about simple honesty. Part of the Mosaic law prescribes: "Ye shall do no unrighteousness . . . in weight, or in measure" (Leviticus 19:35). The Book of Proverbs continues: "A false balance is abomination to the Lord: but a just weight is his delight" (11:1). Merchants used to weigh their produce with weights and balances. Probably everyone has heard the story of the butcher who used to weigh his hand along with the meat. To such deception God thunders an emphatic "No! A pound must weigh a full pound! You must deal with everyone justly and fairly!"

David asked: "Lord, who shall abide in thy tabernacle? Who shall dwell in thy holy hill?" (Psalm 15:1). The answer came: "He that walketh uprightly, and worketh righteousness, and speaketh the truth in his heart . . . He that putteth not out his money to usury, nor taketh reward against the innocent" (verses 2, 5). Here the way of life that pleases God is described in very simple, practical terms: doing what is right, speaking the truth (first of all in our own hearts), and avoiding anything the least bit shady.

The word *faithfulness*, which appears so often in the Old Testament, may also be translated *truth*. God's truth and faithfulness endure through every generation (Psalm 100:5). His word is truth (Psalm 119:142, 160; Revelation 22:6). The Lord is the God of truth (Isaiah 65:16). Christ is "he that is true" (Revelation 3:7), "the faithful and true witness" (Revelation 3:14).

The whole Bible demands basic uprightness and honesty. We often excuse minor lapses from the truth, but Jesus warned, "He who is faithful in a very little is faithful also in much; and he who is dishonest in a very little is dishonest also in much" (Luke 16:10 RSV).

Out of this fundamental requirement for total honesty come three valuable keys to freer, happier, more productive living.

Key Number One: Be Honest with Yourself

David, who knew what it was like to fall into sin and bitterly regret it, wrote: "Behold, thou desirest truth in the inward parts" (Psalm 51:6). All of us have an almost limitless capacity for self-deception. If you doubt that, look at Jeremiah 17:9: "The heart is deceitful above all things, and desperately wicked: who can know it?" The Bible is referring here to hearts in general. There is within each human being a fascination with evil that we seldom admit to, but instead cover up.

Jesus said: "From within, out of the heart of men, proceed evil thoughts, adulteries, fornications, murders, thefts, covetousness . . . an evil eye, blasphemy, pride, foolishness" (Mark 7:21–22). Who can read that list without admitting to possessing at least a few of those qualities? Jesus came to save us from all such wrongdoing and deception.

The poet Robert Burns was sitting in church one day when his eye caught something unusual about the lady sitting in front of him. She was dressed beautifully, and she was naturally beautiful, and she knew it! She was wearing a brand-new balloon-shaped bonnet—across which the poet observed a fat gray louse, plump as a gooseberry, slowly crawling.

The result was Burns' famous poem "To a Louse—on Seeing One on a Lady's Bonnet in Church." It ends with the wise prayer:

> O wad some Power the giftie gie us
> To see oursels as ithers see us!
> It wad from mony a blunder free us,
> An' foolish notion . . .

When we learn to see ourselves as we really are, in total honesty toward ourselves and God, we take a very important step toward more successful living.

Such candid self-appraisal helps us get rid of harmful crutches. A crutch is a fine thing for a while if you have a broken leg—but if you hang on to that crutch too long, you can seriously weaken yourself.

Crutches widely used today are drugs and alcohol. At a reception I met a man who was slightly wobbly after several cocktails and realized he was under the influence.

"Why do I do this?" he asked. "Actually," he answered himself, "I don't really like booze. But I have a shy streak, and a few cocktails loosen me up. I'm just no good socially without the lift I get from alcohol."

Probably many people drink or use drugs for similar reasons. But it is foolish to hobble around on such crutches. To be a good conversationalist, for example, all you need is to take a real interest in drawing other people out.

The Bible is relevant to all our problems, including addiction. Chapter 23 of the Book of Proverbs contains a very realistic description of the alcoholic:

> Show me someone who drinks too much, who has to try out fancy drinks, and I will show you someone miserable and sorry for himself, always causing trouble and always complaining. His eyes are bloodshot, and he has bruises that could have been avoided. Don't let wine tempt you . . . The next morning you will feel as if you had been bitten by a poisonous snake. Weird sights will appear before your eyes, and you will not be able to think or speak clearly. You will feel as if you were out on the ocean, seasick, swinging high up in the rigging of a tossing ship. "I must have been hit," you will say; "I must have have been beaten up, but I don't remember it. Why can't I wake up? I need another drink."
>
> Proverbs 23:29–35 TEV

Many a recovered addict would agree that during his former way of life he was indeed often "miserable and sorry for himself, causing trouble and complaining"—blaming his problems on others instead of facing himself honestly.

An addict is truly a crippled personality. But he or she can be completely cured. Many of us have seen astonishing recoveries through Alcoholics Anonymous. The first one of AA's famous twelve steps is complete honesty: "We admitted we were powerless over alcohol." The other steps in the program all include the same candor. God's power is always available to heal and transform, but the alcoholic must come to the point where he lays aside all self-deception and depends upon God absolutely.

Not surprisingly, Alcoholics Anonymous itself began with an experience of total honesty. In 1935 an event took place that my near neighbor, Dr. Scott Peck, calls one of the greatest events of the twentieth century. In that year two men met in Akron, Ohio. One was "Dr. Bob," who became such an alcoholic during his twenties that he went to the psychiatrist Carl Jung for help. Dr. Jung told him that his problem was beyond the reach of psychiatry and that only one thing could help him. "Seek a religious conversion," Dr. Jung said. "That is the only thing that can save you."

Dr. Bob followed his prescription. He experienced the miracle of a spiritual rebirth, thereby discovering that the power of God could do what nothing else could. With God's help he was able to stop drinking.

Dr. Bob had a drinking buddy named Bill Wilson. Bill also had a drinking problem, which in his case produced cirrhosis of the liver. When he went to his doctor for help, he was told that medicine could not help him. All his life Bill had put his faith in science. Now he felt he had been worshiping a god that had turned out to be as helpless as a wooden idol. The doctor said the only thing that could help Bill was to stop drinking—and this was the one thing he could not do.

Meeting Dr. Bob in Akron, Bill invited him to a bar, as usual, and was surprised to learn that his friend had stopped drinking. When he asked how, Dr. Bob told him: through the power of God. This was no consolation to Bill, for he did not believe in God. But he had an open mind.

When Bill Wilson was hospitalized soon afterward with no prospect but death before him, he made a desperate, unusual prayer that went something like this: "O God, if there is a God, help me!" And that night, after that honest prayer, Bill felt a wind from beyond space blowing through him and a light from beyond the stars shining into his soul. Somehow he knew that God was there and would help him. And He did help him withdraw completely from his dependence on alcohol.

When the two men got together soon afterward, through a process of trial and error and prayer, they worked out the twelve steps and the basic organization of Alcoholics Anonymous. Notice the basic honesty in the steps:

Step one: We admitted we were powerless over alcohol . . .
Step four: Made a searching and fearless moral inventory of ourselves.
Step five: Admitted to God, to ourselves, and to another human being the exact nature of our wrongs.
Step six: Were entirely ready to have God remove all these defects of character.
Step seven: Humbly asked Him to remove our shortcomings . . .

Step ten: Continued to take personal inventory and when we were
wrong promptly admitted it.

The twelve steps, like the Scriptures, require total honesty not
only with ourselves but also with God and others.

Key Number Two: Be Honest with God

It is absolutely essential for successful living to be totally honest with yourself and with God. All through history, men and women
have followed in the footsteps of Adam and Eve. After breaking the
only commandment God gave them, these first humans, conscious
of their guilt, ran away and hid like children. When God called them
they lied. When He asked them why they had disobeyed, Adam
blamed his wife: "That woman You created, she made me do it."
Eve, of course, blamed the serpent. The sin and evasions of this
pair sent the whole human race into a downward spiral that was
reversed only by the cross.

The habit of blaming someone or something else for our mis-
deeds is still with us. A government official convicted in court said,
"Alcohol made me do it." Recovered addicts learn to acknowledge
their own responsibility for what they do.

In Jesus' parable of the Pharisee and the publican (Luke 18:9–14),
the Pharisee apparently had a lot of good things going in his life.
He prayed and tithed to a fault—but he was not honest before God
about such sins as self-righteousness and despising others.

The publican, on the other hand, was a member of one of the
lowest moral classes of his time. Publicans were men who collected
taxes for the government and made their living out of the extra
money they could pocket on the side; they were universally hated.
But this publican had one great trait. All he dared ask of God was
mercy to a sinner (verse 13). And that was enough. The prayer of
total honesty will win every time.

Jesus' story of how the spiritual seed of God's Word grows in our
hearts, in Luke 8:4–15, recounts the sad fate of three-fourths of the
seed. Some was eaten by birds, some burned up in the sun, some
was choked by weeds. The seed that produced an abundant harvest grew "in an honest and good heart" (verse 15).

> **God knows us through and through.**
> **When we stop trying to hide from Him and let Him**
> **cleanse our inmost thoughts and desires,**
> **we learn to love Him and live worthwhile lives.**

The Bible's story of Job presents the record of a man so exemplary that by Old Testament standards he was "perfect" (Job 1:1). Nevertheless, terrible tragedies struck him one after another. He lost all his wealth, then all his children, then even his health; he was so miserable that he wished he had never been born (3:1–3). During his suffering Job felt so bitter about what happened that his friends accused him of heresy and blasphemy. Job's "comforters" probably wanted to help him, but they took the line that he had brought all his troubles on himself.

Job refused to accept that false load of guilt. He did not know why he had such problems—none of us ever knows that completely—but he did know he had tried hard to be upright, and he said so. And in the end God said that it was Job who had told the truth about Him, not his friends. God honored Job's honesty, in spite of his bitter words of near-blasphemy, and restored his health and wealth. Indeed, "The Lord blessed the latter end of Job more than his beginning" (Job 42:12).

An ancient prayer reminds us of our need:

Almighty God, unto whom all hearts are open, all desires known,
and from whom no secrets are hid,
cleanse the thoughts of our hearts
by the inspiration of Thy Holy Spirit,
that we may perfectly love Thee
and worthily magnify Thy holy name.

God knows us through and through. When we stop trying to hide from Him and let Him cleanse our inmost thoughts and desires, we learn to love Him and live worthwhile lives.

Turn to John 5:2–5, to the story of the lame man whom Jesus met at the pool of Bethesda. After thirty-eight years as a handicapped man, he must have given up nearly all hope. But no case is too hopeless for God. Jesus looked through the man, into his deepest need, and lovingly made him whole. He can do the same for any of us.

The members of Alcoholics Anonymous, as noted above, learn to turn their lives over to a higher power and to admit to God, to themselves, and to one other person the exact nature of their wrongs. Such trust and honesty constitute a vital step forward in the art of living.

Key Number Three: Be Honest with Others

It is important to be absolutely honest with other people. In Jesus' day there were religious professionals who tried to impress people with their religiosity by public praying, almsgiving, and fasting (Matthew 6:1–18). They even disfigured their faces to "appear unto men" to be extra-religious (verse 16). If they had been honest with each other, they would not have gone through all that pretense.

As a student pastor Bruce Larson inquired about a teenage girl who was no longer in church, and he learned she had gone out of town because she was pregnant. When he said he would like to talk with her, the church members said, "Oh no! You're the last person she wants to know what's happened!"

Bruce realized how guilty and remorseful the girl probably felt. But he also realized with a shock that too often the church is the last place where many people are honest about their failures. Through his books and messages Bruce shares the good news that God forgives and forgets, and accepts us completely, when we tell Him who we really are. We should forgive, forget, and accept in exactly the same way.

The apostle Paul is sometimes harshly criticized by those who do not seem to understand his deep concern for Christ and His way. But no one can accuse him of dishonesty. In writing to the Christians at Rome, Paul said he hoped to bring them benefit—but he expected to benefit also from being with them (Romans 1:11–12). He wanted them to learn how to live victoriously, but he admitted that he too sometimes failed to do what he wanted to do, doing instead what he loathed (7:14–19).

Paul was not perfect, but he was honest. "We have renounced disgraceful, underhanded ways," he said; "we refuse to practice cunning or to tamper with God's word, but by the open statement of the truth we would commend ourselves to every man's conscience in the sight of God" (2 Corinthians 4:2 RSV).

When we share honestly with others both our failures and our victories, we have taken another giant step forward toward better living.

Ruth Carter Stapleton came across an unusual example of this when she was speaking at a three-day seminar on the topic "Jesus Christ." Just before the first session, as she was sitting at the back of the auditorium, a short, elderly man sat down beside her and told her why he had come. He said he was not a Christian, but he had awakened out of sleep, two nights before, when a voice out of nowhere said distinctly, "Jesus Christ." Seeing the announcements of the meetings, he felt he had to come. Just as the stranger told her this, Ruth had to go forward to speak. That evening and for three days she spoke about Jesus and His unconditional love—and at every meeting the stranger was present.

At the end, when Ruth invited people to meet with her, the little man was among those who came forward. He told her an amazing story. More than thirty years before, he said, he had gone by boat to another country to work at what he thought would be a good job at a resort hotel. On arrival he found that his only pay for scrubbing the floors, lighting the furnace each morning, and doing other chores would be his room and board. Disillusioned and disgusted at the situation, he decided he would take the next boat home.

The next morning he tried to light the furnace as he had been instructed, but only some of the burners ignited. Since they seemed to be burning well, he turned them up and then went to his room, took his suitcase with all his belongings, and left the hotel for the long voyage home.

He was half a block away when he heard an explosion. Looking back, he saw that the hotel was an inferno, flames and smoke belching from its broken windows. Then he ran to his boat. He never found out how many lives had ended in the explosion.

"I've been running ever since," the man told Ruth Stapleton. For thirty years, he said, he had lived in hell as he thought of the destruction he must have inadvertently wrought. "Do you think," he asked her, "Christ can forgive me for what I did?"

Mrs. Stapleton assured the man that Jesus had died for all the sins of the world, and that He would indeed forgive this awesome misdeed if the man confessed it to Him. The man began to sob as the truth sank in. Then he said, "It's gone." He explained that ever since the day of the explosion he had been plagued with a lump in his throat—and now it was gone, for the first time in three decades, along with his guilt and shame. His honest confession brought about healing within and without.[1]

Rev. William L. Vaswig, who directs a ministry of effective prayer, asks why so many of us keep asking for forgiveness for the same mistakes and habits year after year but are never free. "Why don't we begin groups in our churches," he asks, "where people can be honest, where we can pass the pain as well as the peace, and where we can confess our sins and support each other through sharing and prayer?" Many churches are doing this, founding groups with names such as Sinners Anonymous and Victors Anonymous.

In 1736, when he was twenty-six years old, John Wesley sailed from England to Georgia to preach to the Indians. Two years later he wrote in his journal: *I went to America to convert the Indians; but O! who shall convert me?* Wesley's honest recognition of the weakness of his faith led to a meeting soon afterward in Aldersgate Street, London, when his heart was "strangely warmed" with a fresh commitment to Christ. After this, Wesley led thousands to accept Christ through his energetic and successful preaching.

Jesus promised, "Ye shall know the truth, and the truth shall make you free" (John 8:32). Try to learn the truth about yourself and be absolutely honest with yourself. Then share candidly with your loving Father and with several other people exactly how you are progressing spiritually. You will find yourself enjoying life more and living more successfully in every way as you enter more fully into the freedom and peace and power of the Lord.

For happier, more positive living:

1. Remember that God is concerned that you progress mentally, physically, and spiritually.
2. Determine to be absolutely honest about everything in your life.

3. Be honest with yourself. Take responsibility for your actions. Refuse to blame others for your own mistakes and failures.

4. Get rid of any crutches that prevent your growth.

5. Be honest with God. Come to Him just as you are. He loves us in spite of our failures, not because of our goodness. Talk with Him honestly and naturally, as a child talks to a loving parent.

6. Be honest with others. Find a friend or a small group of people with whom you can share your defeats as well as your victories.

7. Never forget that the truth makes us free from false notions, free from bad habits, free from crippling neuroses and fears, free from the prisons of the past. Walk daily with Christ, who is Himself the Truth.

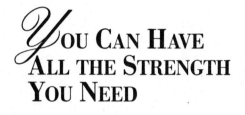

YOU CAN HAVE ALL THE STRENGTH YOU NEED

7

*D*o you ever wish you had more know-how and strength to cope with the problems of life? Do you sometimes feel listless or inadequate? If you do, you are not alone. Many people feel the same way at times. But it is possible to have all the strength you need.

One of the most basic requirements of life is to be strong, both in mind and in body. Simply existing requires a great deal of energy; living a fulfilling life requires much more. When we are strong we can do our work with efficiency and joy.

Garrison Keillor, that gifted entertainer, tells us (tongue in cheek) that Powdermilk Biscuits will give us the strength to get up and do what we need to do. We smile, but he is illustrating a universal fact. Nothing is more disheartening than to feel listless or helpless—and nothing is more important, at such times, than to do something about it. Even the spiritual qualities of faith and love boil down to action: reaching out to God and others.

Many people today are strengthening themselves physically— jogging, walking, running, biking, using exercise equipment, and following sensible diets. This is all to the good. But the most basic and important form of strength is spiritual strength. The Bible is far ahead of current thinking about all this, for two thousand years ago the apostle John wrote, "Beloved, I wish above all things that thou mayest prosper and be in health, even as thy soul prospereth" (3 John 2).

This verse stresses a very practical Bible principle. Both health and prosperity are linked to well-being of the soul and spirit. Without these, health and success are ill founded and cannot bring us real enjoyment.

No wonder the Bible says so much about strength and power. That dynamo of a man, the apostle Paul, knew Christ as "the power of God" (1 Corinthians 1:24). He said that he glorified even in his weaknesses, "that the power of Christ may rest upon me" (2 Corinthians 12:9). He praised the One who "is able to do exceeding abundantly above all that we ask or think" (Ephesians 3:20). He testified to being "strengthened with all might, according to his glorious power" (Colossians 1:11). And what was the secret of the great apostle's seemingly endless energy? Let us ask him. "Thanks be to God," Paul replies, "which giveth us the victory through our Lord Jesus Christ" (1 Corinthians 15:57). Indeed, declares Paul (as we too can affirm today), "I can do all things through Christ who strengthens me" (Philippians 4:13 NKJV).

The great personalities of the Bible were strong individuals. Moses had unusual stamina right down to his hundred and twentieth year (Deuteronomy 34:7). Joseph possessed moral power and political know-how. David was a powerful shepherd, fighter, and king; the Psalms reiterate his confidence in God as his strengthening energizer (Psalms 18:1; 19:14; 28:7–8). The great men and women of faith were people of power who "subdued kingdoms, wrought righteousness, obtained promises, stopped the mouths of lions, quenched the violence of fire, escaped the edge of the sword, out of weakness were made strong" (Hebrews 11:33–34).

Some years ago I came into Cleveland, Ohio, early in the morning on a sleeping-car train to fill a speaking engagement that noonday. A man in the upper berth energetically and quite literally jumped from his berth to the floor. I recognized him as my friend Walter Judd, a famous congressman from Minnesota. He asked, "Where are you speaking today, Norman?"

I told him and we went off together to have breakfast in the station restaurant. "Walter," I said, "you amaze me, batting around on sleeping cars in upper berths and giving speeches every day. You are a dynamo. Where do you get all this energy?"

"From the same source as you. Where do I get my energy? It's simple. I believe what I speak about. And another thing, I believe in God. He wasn't fooling when He said in the Bible, 'Let the weak say, I am strong' [Joel 3:10].

"I've practiced doing just that, and it works," said Congressman Judd, one of the best speakers I have known and one of the most indefatigable. And I must add that I have also practiced that bit of wisdom from the Scriptures and I too find that it works.

Our Lord was and is a power personality. John the Baptist said of Him, "There cometh one mightier than I after me" (Mark 1:7). Even as a child Jesus "waxed strong in spirit" (Luke 1:80). He worked "in the power of the Spirit" (Luke 4:14). He said, "The Son of man hath power on earth to forgive sins" (Matthew 9:6). People "were astonished at this doctrine: for his word was with power" (Luke 4:32). Of course His miracles evinced infinite power. Among His last words before ascending to heaven were, "All power is given unto me in heaven and in earth" (Matthew 28:18).

We too are meant to have power.

Get Rid of Energy-Draining Emotions

When Jesus said, "All power is given unto me," He immediately added, "Go ye therefore. . . . " We do not only have a mighty Christ, we have a Savior who wants and expects you and me also to exercise power. To "as many as received him, to them gave he power" (John 1:12). The first disciples were promised and received that power (Acts 1:8; 19:11; 2 Corinthians 12:12). And we today have access to that same strength.

One way to possess power is to get rid of the emotions that drain energy. Dr. Walter Alvarez, one of the greatest physicians of the twentieth century, once said that one reason he lived to ninety was that he had learned never to get angry or disturbed. The negative emotions—fear, worry, anger, suspicion, and so on—are debilitating. They can consume so much of our energy that we have little or none left. They can ruin our health as well as our energy.

To be strong, learn to be aware of negative feelings when they arise and then consciously say good-bye to them. Replace them with the positive characteristics of trust, confidence, hope, and love. These are sources of power.

Let Go and Let God

A good friend of mine, the late Albert Cliffe of Toronto, Canada, became so ill that his doctors lost hope that he could live. But while he was on that seeming deathbed, Al had a remarkable experience. Bible verses he had heard in his childhood poured into his mind. One of them was: "God is our refuge and strength, a very present help in trouble" (Psalm 46:1).

Suddenly a new realization hit Albert Cliffe like a cyclone. *God is my strength!* he thought. *God is my refuge, God is the strength I need. And God is my present help, right now, in my trouble.* That being so, he concluded, God must be giving him strength right then and there. All he had to do was to receive that gift—to "let go and let God." And those great words *Let Go and Let God* became the title of a valuable book Al wrote explaining how to take possession of the strength God offers.

I realize that while it may sound simple to let go and let God, it is not always easy. Our inner self is an ornery creature that will keep finding reasons why it can't or shouldn't let go. Al Cliffe had to turn away from all that rationalization and say to the Lord, "I am completely in Your hands. Do with me what You will."

Al told me once that in that moment of surrender he felt himself completely separated from all his fears—and they never dominated him again! Accepting God's strength and love, he got up from his sickbed, started a Bible class (which incidentally became the largest in Canada), and began a ministry of speaking and writing that has helped thousands of people find health, energy, and new life.

If you want strength for your daily problems, I urge you to let go of those problems and turn them over to God. Say aloud, "God is my strength." Believe it, utilize the strength you are given, and experience the wondrous flow of His power.

**God is dynamite! He is the most dynamic force
in the world—providing total power
for our needs today and every day.**

Power for the Present

I wrote in chapter 4 about the importance of living in the now. Psalm 46:1 reminds us that God, our refuge and strength, is "a very *present* help in trouble." God gives us power here and now.

Some versions of the Bible give these words as "God is . . . an ever present help." Both translations are correct. God is *very* present today, and *ever* present down through the years. But He is not present in a passive way. He is eager to come into your troubles and difficulties with His answers. All you have to do is to open your mind to Him.

A Bible scholar tells me that in the Greek translation of Psalm 46:1, God is our *dynamis*. This is the source of our words *dynamic* and *dynamite*. God is dynamite! He is the most dynamic force in the world—providing total power for our needs today and every day.

One of the most powerful saints in Christian history is Martin Luther, who revolutionized the church. A profound scholar, Luther knew that the Hebrew word for *refuge* in Psalm 46:1 also means *shelter* or *strong tower* or *fortress*. He also knew that he needed a strong fortress, for the ideas he found in the Bible threatened the established interests of his day, and he was well aware that he might be killed for proclaiming them. Trusting in God for his security and strength, Luther wrote the great hymn "A Mighty Fortress Is Our God" based on the forty-sixth Psalm. Throughout his life of prodigious accomplishments, Luther found Him "a bulwark never failing."

God is our refuge and strength in this century as well as in the sixteenth century A.D. and the centuries B.C. I saw this demonstrated on a train between Chicago and New York. Returning by rail from a meeting in Chicago, I saw a man who seemed to know me, although I didn't remember him. While I was in my compartment trying to do some work, there was a knock on my door. There stood the same man. I invited him in and after a few minutes of talk about the weather, I asked him, "What's on your mind?"

"I don't know," he said. "I'm the CEO of my company, but I'm having trouble." Then he explained that he was having difficulty making decisions. "In my business I have to make many of them," he said, "and often after deciding something, I become fearful that it was the wrong decision." His fear was sapping his strength and his emotional stability.

As he told me this, I noticed there were tears in his eyes. I said, "Here we are on the train together, just the two of us. But Jesus said, where two or three are gathered together in His name, there is He in our midst. So He is here too, riding the rails with us.

"Tell you what," I continued. "Let's talk to the Lord about your problem."

When we finished, the look on this man's face told me he understood how he could get the help he needed. Later I heard he was proving strong, capable, and very successful. He too had found that God is our personal refuge and strength. Here are a few of God's commands about being strong:

> Be strong and of a good courage, fear not, nor be afraid
>   (Deuteronomy 31:6).
> Fear not, nor be dismayed, be strong (Joshua 10:25).
> Be strong and courageous (2 Chronicles 32:7).
> Strengthen ye the weak hands (Isaiah 35:3).
> Watch ye, stand fast in the faith, quit you like men, be strong
>   (1 Corinthians 16:13).
> Be strong in the Lord, and in the power of his might (Ephesians 6:10).

You may ask, how can I be strong? First, remember that God *is* your strength (Psalm 46:1). Give yourself completely to Him, as Al Cliffe did, and receive His strength.

Then, act strong. The more you act that way, the stronger you will get. (The reverse is also true, of course. A healthy person who becomes inactive will soon lose most of his strength.) No matter how weak or inadequate you may feel, do something positive. As you take action—no matter whether the action is physical or spiritual—God's power will flow into you.

Think about that marvelous little creature the hummingbird, which darts from flower to flower faster than the eye can follow. I am told that if a human being were to exert as much energy as a hummingbird he would have to eat between two hundred and four hundred pounds of food a day just to maintain that energy! Fortunately, we can get by with far less intake. But the God who created hummingbirds and human beings gives each one the strength needed to do all He wants us to do.

When we read in Ephesians 6:10, "be strong in the Lord, and in the power of his might," we see an important clue to acquiring the strength we need. The Lord provides the power; all we need to do is to make the right connection. A friend of mine bought an automobile that worked fine until he left the lights on too long after he had parked it. When he went to start his car, he discovered the power was gone. His problem was solved when his son came to his rescue with jumper cables and got his car going again.

My friend realized he had made a mistake. The only thing wrong with his car was that he had let the battery run down. Once he made the right connections, however, the power returned and everything was okay. Believe, and "let go and let God." It's very simple, I grant, but that is what you do to regain power.

God, the Lord, is the Almighty. All power is in Him, in Jesus, and in the Holy Spirit. And we become strong in Him and the power of His might.

For more power in your life, I suggest you read and memorize some of the strong verses from the Bible, such as:

The joy of the Lord is your strength (Nehemiah 8:10).
The Lord is the strength of my life (Psalm 27:1).
The Lord will give strength unto his people (Psalm 29:11).
Cast thy burden upon the Lord, and he shall sustain thee
    (Psalm 55:22).
In quietness and in confidence shall be your strength (Isaiah 30:15).
He giveth power to the faint; and to them that have no might he
    increaseth strength (Isaiah 40:29).
The people that do know their God shall be strong, and shall do
    exploits (Daniel 11:32).

Ye shall receive power (Acts 1:8).

In all these things we are more than conquerors through him that
loved us (Romans 8:37).

The word of God is quick [alive], and powerful (Hebrews 4:12).

My grace is sufficient for thee: for my strength is made perfect in
weakness (2 Corinthians 12:9).

Prescription for Strength

When I was about thirty-five, I had a physician in New York City,
Dr. William S. Bainbridge, a prominent doctor. He was a very strong
man personally and a great physician. He was equally strong in his
faith. He often referred to the Bible as "The Rule Book" of wisdom
and as "the greatest book on health."

About that time I was out of town on a series of speaking engage-
ments every night with a couple of noonday luncheon talks thrown
in. This was before air travel was common, and I usually used sleeping trains. Arriving back in New York early one Saturday, I went
home for breakfast. Then I told Ruth, "I think I'll run over to see
Dr. Bainbridge. I feel a cold coming on. When I come back I'll work
on my sermon for tomorrow. Expect me back in about half an hour."

The doctor, as was his custom, chatted in his easygoing way
before examining me, and I told him about the exciting week that
had just passed.

"Well, let's look at that throat," he said. He took my temperature
and blood pressure, squirted some medicine into my throat and
more up my nostrils and finished by stuffing some medicated pack-
ing in my nose, whereupon he put me in a little room. "Lie down on
that couch and let the medicine work," he said. "Meanwhile, meditate on the good old Bible, the greatest Rule Book known to man."

"You won't keep me long, Bill, will you?" I added, "I've got a ter-
rifically busy day. I have to do a week's paperwork in one day."

"You just lie there and relax," he said and shut the door.

I knew Bill Bainbridge's methods, so I thought of everything I
could remember that the Bible says about health—and it's plenty.
After about an hour the doctor said, "You can come out now. You're
young and we want you strong for the long pull."

I got home considerably later than I had expected, but the combination of medicine and Bible meditation knocked out that cold and provided all the strength I needed for many days afterward.

The apostle Paul prayed that the Christians of Ephesus might be "strengthened with might by his Spirit in the inner man" (Ephesians 3:16). Everything important begins within, in the heart and mind. To be strong and healthy, think strength and health. And let God work deep in your innermost being to increase your spiritual vitality. Out of spiritual growth springs every other seed of health and strength.

There is an important parable about spiritual growth in the Gospel of Luke, chapter 8, verses 4–15. When Jesus said, "A sower went out to sow his seed," He was speaking of something familiar to everyone. Anyone with land plants it in the spring and tends the crops with great care until the harvest. The Bible is full of references to planting, cultivating, weeding, protecting from marauders, and finally the joy of the harvest. A great many of Jesus' parables are based on this fundamental activity.

With that in mind, I suggest you look up Luke 8:4–15 and ask yourself: What were the four kinds of places the seed fell into? What happened to the seed in each of these places? You might say these four areas represent the closed mind, the shallow mind, the overcrowded mind, and the productive mind!

Now, the most important question of all: What does Jesus' story mean for our spiritual growth? Fortunately, the Lord's first hearers asked the same question (verse 9). And His answer, in verses 11 through 14, gives vital clues to obtaining abundant growth.

"The seed is the word of God" (verse 11). What God says to us is the seed that can produce a spiritual harvest in our lives. The effort you give to the Bible, the time you spend in daily devotions, may seem unnecessary. But the fact is that every time you listen carefully to a truth of the Lord, you are strengthening your spirit for the problems and conflicts of life.

Fill your mind with God's Word, do what He says, and you will be prepared for anything, for you will reap a spiritual harvest.

Seven Steps to Greater Strength

God's Word can bring you a hundredfold harvest (Luke 8:8). That's an enviable return on any investment! But to receive that abundant blessing, you must do your part. Here are seven steps:

1. *Preparation.* Seed cannot grow on hard, unprepared soil. We can prepare for our growth by making sure that God's Word lodges in "honest and good" hearts (Luke 8:15). We need to be absolutely honest with ourselves and God. And we must turn away completely from whatever is harmful or evil.

2. *Planting.* Do we think about what God says in the Bible, or do we forget what we read? One way to plant the seed of God's truth firmly in our hearts is to write down what He tells us there and read it over and over, repeating it and thinking about it until it becomes a part of our lives.

3. *Feeding.* Seed needs "good soil" for nutrition. Do we feed our minds with negative, destructive thoughts, or are we willing to concentrate on what is "true . . . pure . . . lovely . . . of good report" (Philippians 4:8)? Do we practice the attitude of gratitude? The more we think positively, the better God's words can grow within us.

4. *Cultivating.* Cultivating breaks up the soil so water and air can get to a plant's roots and it can flourish. Probably cultivating is not a very pleasant experience for the plant. If its roots could feel, they might be very upset at being disturbed! And surely the pruning or "purging" that a gardener must give a grapevine is painful, but it is necessary, and it produces fruitfulness (John 15:2).

So when change comes to us, we can thank God that He may be preparing the way for us to live more abundantly.

5. *Weeding.* Luke 8:14 tells us that the seed that fell among thorns and weeds represents those who are "choked with cares and riches and pleasures of this life."

Cares sometimes become worries. Worry can choke the life out of you, physically as well as spiritually. Don't let it destroy you. Cast all your cares on the Lord, for He cares deeply for you (1 Peter 5:7).

Riches can distract us from the true values of life. So can pleasures. Both these things, while good in themselves, can stunt our spiritual life if we let them crowd out God's Word. Ruthlessly weed out of your life whatever chokes your mental and spiritual growth.

6. *Persisting.* A friend told me recently, "Every year I enjoy planting some vegetables in our community gardens. In the spring, when the whole field is freshly plowed and planted, how neat everything looks! But by late summer you wouldn't believe the difference. Some of the gardens are bearing tomatoes, corn, and various vegetables. But quite a number of them are hopeless masses of towering weeds. The gardeners who kept up with the hoeing and weeding have beautiful gardens. Those who got behind and quit lost everything in the weeds."

It can well be said about the gardens of our hearts, "He who endures to the end will be saved" (Matthew 24:13 RSV). Jesus concludes His story with the words, "But that on the good ground are they, which in an honest and good heart, having heard the word, keep it, and bring forth fruit with patience" (Luke 8:15). Note the words *keep* and *patience.* Keep with the best, keep at what God wants you to do with patient endurance, and His fruitfulness will bless your life.

7. *Harvesting.* What is that fruitfulness? From John 15:1–16 we may conclude that it is love, joy, and answered prayer (verses 10, 11, 16). And the Lord wants us to become "fruitful in every good work" (Colossians 1:10). You can be sure that if you follow the steps to spiritual growth, you will find yourself strengthened within, ready for the good things God wants you to do—and enjoy.

For a summary of the harvest we can expect, turn to Galatians 5:22–23. Today's English Version of the Bible puts it this way: "But the Spirit produces love, joy, peace, patience, kindness, goodness, faithfulness, humility, and self-control." With those qualities abounding within, you will have all the strength you need to cope with whatever life brings.

For greater strength mentally, physically, and spiritually:

1. Utilize the immense power of faith.
2. Get rid of energy-draining emotions.

3. Fill your life with the positive characteristics of trust, confidence, hope, and love.
4. Let go and let God work.
5. Use the strength you have and you will gain more.
6. Give yourself a spiritual checkup.
7. For increasing power, follow God's principles of growth.

THE POWER OF HOPE

8

If things aren't working out right for you, perhaps you are not working things right. Is it possible you are neglecting one of the most important forces available? The greatest thing in the world, the Bible assures us in 1 Corinthians 13:13, is love. But the second and third greatest things—powers that will last forever, in contrast to so much that is here today and gone tomorrow—are faith and hope. Hope is an indispensable part of our spiritual equipment.

When I was a small boy, my brother Bob and I sometimes visited our grandparents in Lynchburg, Ohio, for a few days. One night, just as Grandma had put us to bed, a terrible storm came up. A great wind shook the house. Lightning flashed and thunder rolled while the rain hurled itself in great sheets against the windowpanes. From the bed I could see the huge maple tree outside our windows lashing back and forth in the fury of the storm. I was terrified. I said to Bob, "That tree will never last this out. It's going to go down."

Both of us jumped out of bed and scurried downstairs to where Grandma was reading by a kerosene lamp. When we told her our fears, she bundled us up and took us out on the porch. "There's nothing to be afraid of," she said. "God is in the rain and the storm. That tree is having a good time with the wind. See how it bends?

The tree doesn't fight the wind, it cooperates with it by bending back and forth. I think it will be there for a long time. Now you boys go back to bed. Remember that God is in this storm, and all storms ultimately pass."

A few years ago I went back to Lynchburg and stood again under that same tree. Storms come and go, but the old maple is still there, laughing at the storms. A great tree can ride out a violent storm because it sends its roots down deep into the earth.

When people crash from the storms of life, it may be because they don't have the right root system. Send down into the soil of your life the three great roots of faith, hope, and love, and nothing in this world can destroy you.

Did you ever see a two-legged stool? Years ago farmers often sat on three-legged stools when they milked their cows. But a stool with only two legs wouldn't work! Make sure you deepen your hope as well as your faith and your love, and you will become indomitable.

The fact is, "we are saved by hope" (Romans 8:24). That truth came home to me when I read a news story about a man caught in a Midwestern blizzard. The snow was so deep that his car was stalled in the drifts several miles from his home. He left the car and started to walk home. He almost got there.

But apparently this man gave up too soon. He managed to get almost home—but he must have thought he was hopelessly lost, for the next morning his frozen body was found only a few hundred feet from his house. If he had kept on, in hope, for only a few minutes more, he would have made it. He would have been saved by hope.

To appreciate how important hope is, think of what happens when a person loses it. The result? The eight dreadful D words: dismay, discouragement, distrust, disinterest, depression, despair, defeat, disaster.

You may think that is putting it too strongly, but the evidence is increasing every day that the positive attitudes of the Bible produce confidence, happiness, health, and well-being, while negative attitudes such as cynicism, anger, and irritation destroy not only good relationships but also physical, financial, and emotional stability.

Scientific Evidence of the Power of Hope

The science section of the *New York Times* for December 24, 1991, contained an article by Daniel Goleman with the title "Hope Emerges as Key to Success in Life." He said:

> Psychologists are finding that hope plays a surprisingly potent role in giving people a measurable advantage in realms as diverse as academic achievement, bearing up in onerous jobs, and coping with tragic illness. And, by contrast, the loss of hope is turning out to be a stronger sign that a person may commit suicide than other factors long thought to be more likely risks.[1]

The article reported on a number of studies regarding the importance of hope in practical life. One of these was done by Dr. Charles R. Snyder, a psychologist at the University of Kansas who measures the correlation between hope and good grades. "Hope has proven a powerful predictor of outcome," he says. He and other psychologists are trying to teach children the ways of thinking that hopeful people possess.

Norman Cousins did considerable research on the power of positive emotions such as joy, laughter, and hope. His book *Head First: The Biology of Hope* relates his ten years in the medical community, particularly on the faculty of the School of Medicine of the University of California. Cousins held the only honorary degree in medicine awarded at the Yale University School of Medicine. *Head First* presents massive scientific evidence of the harmful effects of the negative emotions and emphasizes the power of hope, faith, and love to enhance healing.

A psychiatrist at Massachusetts General Hospital, Joel Dimsdale, became curious about the characteristics of the people who had managed to survive Nazi death camps during World War II. Interviewing a number of these survivors, Dr. Dimsdale found one element that towered above everything else. One prisoner had focused on the prospect of rejoining her family. Another looked forward to getting out into the sunshine in the prison yard on the next sunny day. Another prisoner set a goal for himself of lasting until the next Hanukkah. Almost all these survivors held to one form or another of "blind, naked hope." Throwing their thoughts into the future, they used hope like a magnet to draw them to safety.[2]

> **Just as faith looks up, hope looks confidently forward and grasp the future.**

What Is Hope?

Check any reference work to see how often the Bible speaks of the importance of hope. But do not be misled by some present-day, watered-down definition of that quality. When a person says "I hope so," he may be just vaguely wishing something were better. In contrast, the hope the Bible offers is something solid and strong. The great Bible scholar Joseph H. Thayer says it means "joyful and confident expectation" that what God promises will become ours. Another scholar, Alexander Cruden, calls hope "a firm expectation of all promised good things."

In *The New Bible Dictionary* J. D. Douglas says that hope means believing that God is blessing us now and will continue to do so. Our hope, he writes, "is not a kite at the mercy of the changing winds, but an 'anchor of the soul, both sure and steadfast,' penetrating deep into the invisible eternal world (Hebrews 6:19)."

Very simply, we might say that just as faith looks up, hope looks confidently forward and grasps the future. Did you ever ride a bicycle? If you have, you know that you can't stay upright unless you are moving ahead. The minute you stop moving, you lose your balance! Maybe that is why some retirees seem to run down and collapse when they leave their jobs. But those who turn retirement into readjustment, who use their new leisure to do new things, keep strong and healthy and young in spirit. Hope is the forward-looking spirit of optimism, of setting goals and finding a purpose.

Henry Thoreau wrote in his great book *Walden:* "I learned this at least by my experiment: that if one advances confidently in the direction of his dreams, and endeavors to live that life which he has imagined, he will meet with a success unexpected in common hours."

Martin Luther said: "Everything that is done in the world is done by hope. No farmer would sow one grain of corn if he hoped not it would grow up and become seed; no bachelor would marry a wife if he hoped not to have children; no merchant or tradesman would set himself to work if he did not hope to reap benefit thereby."

The theologian Emil Brunner wrote: "What oxygen is to the lungs, such is hope for the meaning of life." And that upbeat lyricist Oscar Hammerstein II says, "Reality is as beautiful as it is ugly. . . . I just couldn't write anything without hope in it."

What Hope Can Do for Us

Hope Is a Powerful Motivator

"Faith is the substance of things hoped for" (Hebrews 11:1). Abraham was not only a man of great faith but also a man of great hope: Romans 4:18 tells us that he "against hope believed in hope, that he might become the father of many nations." Looking forward, he hoped and believed that what God had promised would come true. And his hope was rewarded: Through the birth of Isaac he saw the beginning of the multitude he was to father. Still, while on earth, Abraham was a nomad, simply camping out in the Land of Promise, but "he looked for a city which hath foundations, whose builder and maker is God" (Hebrews 11:10).

In 1989 Jane Pauley interviewed the great opera singer Jessye Norman on the Today show. Jane said, "You must have come from an unusual home."

"Yes," Jessye said, "I was born in Augusta, Georgia, and we children were taught early on what the world is really like. We were told that we must work very hard and that we could become anything we wanted to be. We believed this propaganda," Jessye smiled.

Such a down-to-earth philosophy has nerved millions of men and women to accomplish marvelous things. It is a philosophy of hope buttressed by faith and hard work.

Elbert Hubbard wrote these important words about the motivational power of hope: "Try to fix firmly in your mind what you would like to do, and as the days go gliding by, you will find yourself unconsciously seizing upon the opportunities that are required for the fulfillment of your desire.

"Picture in your mind the able, earnest, useful person you desire to be, and the thought you hold is hourly transforming you into that particular individual.

"Thought is supreme. Preserve a right mental attitude—the attitude of courage, frankness, and good cheer. To think rightly is to create. All things come through desire and every sincere prayer is answered. We become like that on which our thoughts are fixed."

Hope Can Get Us through Great Difficulties

Looking for God in dark moments sustains hope (Lamentations 3:21–24). One summer my friend Lloyd Ogilvie was vacationing on the rugged coast of Scotland. Late one afternoon, he recounts in his book *A Future and a Hope,* he set out on a long hike without telling anyone where he was going. It was raining, as it often does in Scotland, but Lloyd plunged ahead enjoying the brisk wind and the crash of the waves on the rocks.

He was soon on those rocks, jumping from one boulder to another, when his foot slipped on a wet surface and his leg caught between two giant boulders. When he managed to get it out, it collapsed beneath him "like limp spaghetti." He could not put any weight on it. (Later he learned his leg was broken in seven places.) He also realized that he was several miles from human habitation and that he could very well die in the cold before anyone started looking for him.

Lloyd Ogilvie prayed. A plan came to him. He discovered that he could move slowly by pushing himself backward with his hands over the wet rocks, like a crippled crab. But he was in such pain that he sometimes blacked out. From time to time he shouted, but no one answered. He wondered if he would make it.

At one of his worst moments, there in the bitter cold of the Scottish coast, there raced across Lloyd's mind a verse he had memorized years before:

> For I know the thoughts which I think toward you, says the Lord, thoughts of peace and not of evil, to give you a future and a hope.
>
> Jeremiah 29:11 NKJV

Lloyd felt that the Lord was telling him personally: "I'm going to give you a future and a hope. You are not finished! *I am your Hope!*"

Soon after that it stopped raining. Then Lloyd saw three people walking in the distance. They turned out to be a doctor and his children who had decided to take a walk when the rain stopped. The doctor summoned a Land Rover from a farmer and got Lloyd to a hospital where he was treated. Out of that experience Lloyd Ogilvie developed a stronger hope and a deeper assurance of God's presence in his life.

Hope Carries Us toward Our Goals

One of America's up-and-coming young businessmen was born on the Ivory Coast of Africa. Remy Toh was not satisfied, however, with the prospect of spending his life like his countrymen. Looking at magazines such as *Ebony,* he determined to become like one of the successful people pictured there. His hope was clear and focused.

Remy decided to come to America, even though he knew the way would be long and hard. *I'll get there and make something of myself,* he vowed, *even if I kill myself trying.*

During his teen years Remy Toh had to quit school and go to work, but he held on to his dream. After two years of saving everything he could, he had enough money to fly to France. There he had to work and save for six more years before he could buy a ticket to New York.

Toh was disillusioned by the slums of New York City, and even more so by the attitude of the workers on his first job in this country. None of them seemed able to think in higher terms than working the rest of their lives in a bakery.

But Toh didn't let himself feel defeated. He took three jobs, sometimes working ninety hours a week. Employment at a modeling agency gave him an idea for a business of his own. But to start it, he had to invest $1500 he had saved and then persuade a bank to lend him $25,000.

Today, still in his early thirties, Toh is president of his own company, W & W Productions. From his Manhattan office he provides a variety of entertainment and business services. He may not yet be famous, but through the power of a focused hope, he is on the way.

Hope Sustains When All Else Fails

Rocky Lyons, five-year-old son of football star Marty Lyons, was fast asleep beside his mother as she drove their pickup truck. He was jolted wide awake. Something terrible was happening. The truck had hit a giant pothole and shot off the road, rolling and bouncing to the bottom of a forty-foot ravine.

"Get away, Rocky," mother Kelley Lyons cried when everything crashed to sudden silence. She couldn't see—blood from dozens of cuts filled her eyes—and she thought she was blind. She was afraid the truck would explode. The boy obediently pushed open the door and scrambled a few feet away.

Then Rocky came right back. He took in the whole nightmarish scene. His mom's hands were still gripping the steering wheel of the smashed truck, her head and dress covered with blood.

Rocky realized exactly what he had to do. *I've got to get her out of there*, he thought, *and get her to a hospital.*

"Come on, Mom," Rocky said as he tugged her door open. "I can help you get up the hill." He wheedled and pushed and pulled, and the two slowly crept up through the tangled underbrush.

Halfway up the steep bank, Mrs. Lyons was exhausted. "I can't go any farther, Rocky," she said. "You go on."

"Oh, Mom," said Rocky, "think of the little train—'I think I can, I think I can.'" *The Little Engine That Could* was his favorite story. He kept tugging and encouraging until they got the rest of the way up the bank to the highway, where a passing driver took them to the hospital. Mrs. Lyons, whose injuries included two broken shoulders, is sure she would have died without her son's help. What he did is an astounding example of the power of hope that refuses to give in.[3]

Naval Captain Gerald L. Coffee was flying over the China Sea in 1966 when his plane was shot down. He spent the next seven years in prison camps in various parts of Vietnam.

For a long time the captain heard nothing from home. He writes in his book *Beyond Survival* that he wondered what was happening to his wife and children. Finally he got a letter from his wife filled with news from home—but it included a strange sentence: *"The boys swim and dive off the dock, and little Jerry splashes around with a little [plastic] bubble on his back."*

Coffee wondered, *Who's little Jerry?* Then he realized the dismaying truth: His wife's previous letters had never reached him. A new son had been born while the captain was in Vietnam, but this was the first word he had received about him. Little Jerry was growing up without his father! The captain's eyes filled with tears.

After seven seemingly endless years, Commander Coffee—promoted two whole ranks while he was a prisoner of war—was released and flown home. Attending church with his family, he responded to the parish priest's welcome with these words:

> Faith was really the key to my survival all those years. Faith in myself
> ... my fellow man ... my comrades in prison ... And of course, faith
> in my God—truly, as all of you know, the foundation for it all.[4]

What techniques of faith did Commander Coffee use to survive those awful years as a prisoner? On Sundays the men passed a signal—"church call" and recited the twenty-third Psalm: "The Lord is my shepherd; I shall not want . . . thou preparest a table before me in the presence of mine enemies . . . my cup runneth over." After his release Coffee said the words helped him realize that the Lord was with him, that his cup of blessings was running over, that someday he would return to his home and his homeland.

Commander Coffee and other prisoners also played a game of imagination while they awaited release. They pictured each room in their home and visualized what it would be like to be going back there.

What pulled these men through was the power of hope.

Be a Faith-Filled Optimist

Please read in your Bible Hebrews 11:6. Underline or write down and commit to memory these important words:

> For he that cometh to God must believe that he is, and that he is a
> rewarder of them that diligently seek him.

Pessimism is the outlook that things are terrible and are going to get worse. It is really unbelief. Optimism believes (as Hebrews 11:6 explains), first, that there is a good God, and second, that He will and does reward those who trust Him enough to seek Him and to do His will. John Calvin wrote, "The word *hope* I take for faith; and indeed hope is nothing else but the constancy of faith."

In the book *Bible Wisdom for Modern Living*, the Reverend David Brown lists outstanding Scriptures illustrating vital topics. Under "Optimism" he provides these inspiring verses from the Revised Standard Version:

> May all who seek thee
>   rejoice and be glad in thee!
> May those who love thy salvation
>   say evermore, "God is great!"
>
> Psalm 70:4

> I will hope continually,
>   and will praise thee yet more and more.
>
> Psalm 71:14

> Rejoice in your hope.
>
> Romans 12:12

If words such as these take control of your mind and your attitude toward life, you will become an in-depth optimist.

Think of any great personality of the Bible. Did Moses cower at the challenge of freeing his countrymen from slavery in Egypt? Not after God filled his life! Although Moses was initially rather pessimistic about his abilities, God led him to the point where he inspired thousands to travel through many difficulties to the Promised Land. (The story is told in the early chapters of the Book of Exodus.) Were Abraham, Joseph, Daniel, and Paul optimists or pessimists? Once God touched their lives, each of these individuals exhibited a remarkable ability to face the hardest problems with the can-do attitude of courage and confidence.

I am impressed by the outstanding book *The Power of Optimism* by Alan Loy McGinnis.[5] One of the important points he makes is that true optimism is not a soft-headed closing of one's eyes to unpleasant facts, but rather a recognition that although the world is imperfect, we can do something about our problems. Here are some of McGinnis' suggestions:

1. *Think of yourself as a problem solver.* A survey of the world's top managers showed that one thing they had in common was a refusal to think or talk failure. Believe that you can cope with your difficulty, and you will.

2. *Look for multiple options.* If one approach doesn't work, the optimist finds another. Thomas Edison might have been discouraged after hundreds of experiments failed to produce a usable electric light bulb. Instead, he said: "We now know a thousand things that won't work, so we're that much closer to finding one that will." And soon afterward he put together the one combination of elements that worked.

3. *Talk freely about your negative feelings.* Don't let them fester inside; admit your feelings and then get beyond them. In 1953 George and Barbara Bush were deeply concerned when they learned that their three-year-old daughter Robin had leukemia. Barbara's hair began turning white. George and Barbara shared their grief. She said, "George held me tight and wouldn't let go. You know, [many] people who lose their children get divorced because one doesn't talk to the other. He did not allow that."

4. *Look for the good in bad situations.* The great writer C. S. Lewis was devastated when his wife, Joy, died. He told about his loss in the remarkable book *A Grief Observed.* Not only has this book helped many people who have lost a loved one, but writing it helped Lewis work through his sorrow. Great good emerged from a very difficult situation.

McGinnis says that tough-minded optimists have certain important characteristics. A few of those characteristics are:

> Optimists are seldom surprised by trouble.
> Optimists believe they have control over their future.
> Optimists heighten their powers of appreciation.

How do you measure up against these characteristics? If there are some areas of your life in which you feel your faith and hope are weak, work on them. As you grow in hope-filled optimism, you will find yourself happier, stronger, and a greater blessing to everyone you meet.

Our Best Hope Is in God

Hope that helps is not centered merely in things but in spiritual realities, in the Lord. He is our ultimate Hope, in this world and in the world to come. "If in this life only we have hope in Christ, we are of all men most miserable" (1 Corinthians 15:19). But that horrible "if" is followed in the next sentence by a mighty "but": "But now is Christ risen from the dead." The Lord of Hope who is with us now will be ours forever.

> Be of good courage, and he shall strengthen your heart, all ye that hope in the Lord (Psalm 31:24).
> Happy is he . . . whose hope is in the Lord his God (Psalm 146:5).

You may have to struggle to hope. But it is an upward struggle, and when struggle is upward, the end is always victory.

There is a massive church in Detroit on Woodward Avenue, the main street of the great motor city. On the lawn in front of the church there is one statue—not a statue of a saint, nor a famous religious figure, but of a seemingly nameless man about forty years of age.

The church is the Metropolitan United Methodist, and it was built by a popular preacher, Dr. Merton S. Rice, who preached there for some twenty-five years to packed crowds.

One Sunday during one of our economic recessions when the attitude of hope for the future was at a premium, Dr. Rice preached an unforgettable sermon on hope. There was that day, in the overflowing congregation of discouraged people, a notable artist. He was so impressed by the sensible and positive message of undefeated faith and hope that he hurried to his studio. And he molded the statue that stands alone on the church lawn.

It depicts a man struggling in adversity, his muscles straining with exertion to overcome. His face contains the light of victory. The entire figure is straining upward with hope.

On the base of the statue is inscribed the Scripture upon which Dr. Rice's sermon was based: "Why art thou cast down, O my soul? and why art thou disquieted within me? hope thou in God: for I shall yet praise him, who is the health of my countenance, and my God" (Psalm 42:11).

To make better use of the power of hope:

1. Begin utilizing the indispensable power of hope in your daily life.
2. Let hope draw you like a magnet toward your goal.
3. If things look hopeless, remind yourself that God wants to give you "a future and a hope."
4. Become a faith-filled optimist.
5. Think hope, verbalize hope, pray with hope, live hope.
6. Let God's words of hope lead you forward into the wonderful future He has in store for you.

MULTIPLY YOUR BLESSINGS

9

y prayer for you, as you read this book, is that you may find the joy and excitement of positive living—and that you may experience it *abundantly* (John 10:10). The Good News Bible translates that statement of Jesus: "I have come in order that you might have life—life in all its fullness." This is what faith is all about! God made us and Jesus saves us so we can have life to the fullest—spiritually, intellectually, emotionally, and physically.

Jesus said that life is like a vine bearing no fruit, some fruit, or much fruit (John 15:1–5). He spoke of seed that never grew and of other seed that did, some multiplying itself thirty times, some sixty times, some a hundred times (Mark 4:2–8). And the apostle Peter wrote: "Grace unto you, and peace, be multiplied" (1 Peter 1:2).

It is possible to live without God's blessing. It is possible to receive only a little of it. No doubt most of us would like His blessing in abundance! And when we remove the obstacles, when we let God love us, His gifts are like a cornucopia of good things "pressed down, and shaken together, and running over" (Luke 6:38). We are promised that "no good thing will he withhold from them that walk uprightly" (Psalm 84:11).

Recently I received a letter from Mrs. Jean Knight of Lubbock, Texas, describing the severely depressed condition she had long endured. Although her home seemed like "a model home," her religious ideas were negative, and inwardly she grew listless and hopeless. In spite of psychiatry, medication, and even shock treatments, she lost weight and sleep; she was miserable and lonely.

Then a friend influenced her to practice some of the principles of positive thinking. Suspicious at first, she thought, *But what do I have to lose?* Then, as she absorbed some of the ideas you will find in this book, Jean wondered if she dared to believe not only in God but also in herself. Would Christ give me strength, she asked herself, by just affirming Philippians 4:13? She writes:

> My faith was weak, but it was enough for Christ. He gave me all the strength my small amount of faith could handle. Slowly but surely, I came back from the living dead . . .
>
> Today I have so much to be thankful for, and thank God every day for life itself! My life is creative and productive, and I feel happiness every day. Thirteen years ago, I started a business from scratch with no capital and little formal education, and our sales are now over a million dollars annually. My children are all Christians, and I have a wonderful husband. But it all came about after I began to use Positive Thinking.

Some difference, moving from "the living dead" to vibrant life! But experiencing that life is possible for anyone.

Would you like to receive God's abundant blessings—definite blessings, increased blessings, multiplied blessings? Then come with me on a little adventure in spiritual arithmetic.

What to Subtract from Your Life

In Peter's First Epistle we learn how this comes about. In the first three verses of the second chapter, God tells us to "lay aside," or subtract from our lives, "all malice, and all guile, and hypocrisies, and envies, and all evil speakings." In other words, say good-bye to wrong attitudes—to ill will, insincerity, pretense, jealousy, recrimination, gossip, and anything else lurking in your heart that is not 100 percent in line with the loving, perfect will of God. Refuse to let those negative things spoil your life!

Recently a friend told me of an experience that shows one way this can take place. Dan, as I'll call him, stopped one day at the drive-in window of a fast-food restaurant for a sandwich. "When I got my change," Dan said, "I couldn't believe it. I said to the cashier, 'I gave you a twenty-dollar bill, not a ten.'"

"Are you sure?" the girl asked.

"Absolutely!" said Dan with such conviction that the cashier handed him another ten-dollar bill. He drove away, pleased that he hadn't been shortchanged.

But when Dan opened his wallet later, there was a twenty-dollar bill—possibly the one he thought he had given the cashier. Since Dan tries to be absolutely honest, he went back to the restaurant the next day and talked to the manager. "Were you short yesterday?" Dan asked. The manager said that his receipts had indeed been off by ten dollars. Dan explained how he thought he might have inadvertently been the cause and gave him the ten dollars.

"The manager was flabbergasted," Dan told me. "He let me know that he didn't believe one person in a million would be that scrupulous. But as I drove away, I felt great. And that very day my son [who had undergone extensive surgery, and for whom a number of people had been praying] showed definite improvement."

If you make a sincere effort to live with God and try to square your life with His Word, eliminating whatever you know is wrong, you have taken a giant step toward multiplied spiritual blessings. And often toward down-to-earth material blessings, too.

What to Add

Let's move on from the negative to the positive, from subtraction to addition. The Old Testament is full of "do nots," but the New Testament emphasis is on "do!" And God wants us to *add* certain things to our faith.

In his Second Epistle, Peter again says, "Grace and peace be multiplied unto you" (2 Peter 1:2). Now look at the next few verses (5–7). Faith, as Peter knew so well, is the beginning of every good thing. But for multiplied blessing, faith needs to grow. And for that to happen, we need to add seven important characteristics.

1. *Excellence.* In 2 Peter 1:5 we are told to add virtue to our faith. In the ancient Greek world *virtue* meant excellence, or simple goodness or soundness. God wants us to excel! We should be *good* at whatever we do. Forget the snide comments you may hear about "do-gooders" or "being goody-goody." For breakfast, would you rather have a good egg or a bad egg? Would you rather send your child to a bad school or a good one?

For better, happier living, make excellence your aim. And don't be afraid of simple goodness. Jesus "went about doing good" (Acts 10:38). He commands us, "Let your light so shine before men, that they may see your good works, and glorify your Father which is in heaven" (Matthew 5:16).

2. *Knowledge.* God did not give us brains to remain empty, nor to fill with worthless trivia. We need to use our heads. Peter's First Epistle tells us, "Gird up the loins of your mind" (1:13). Just as an athlete in ancient times prepared for action by tucking his robe into a belt around his hips so he would be free to move, we must roll up our mental sleeves so we can think clearly. President Lyndon B. Johnson once observed, "A man's judgment is no better than the information he gets." When we learn all we can, we are that much better equipped to do what God wants us to do.

God's blessings are multiplied in our lives particularly "through the knowledge of God, and of Jesus our Lord" (2 Peter 1:2). A truly happy life is not based on simply knowing a lot. It comes from knowing the greatest Friend we can ever have. How do you know a person? By getting acquainted with him, spending some time with him, learning what he thinks and how he reacts to different circumstances. It is the same with knowing the Lord. Take time for Him. Learn from your own experience how wonderful He is. And your blessings will be abundantly multiplied.

3. *Self-control.* We must add to our knowledge temperance (2 Peter 1:6). This really means self-control. All of us are bundles of instincts, impulses, and desires that need firm control if we are to rise above the level of babyhood. An infant's world is governed

by its basic needs and emotions. If the child does not learn to control its urges, it will never be able to function in a civilized world.

It is possible to be controlled by a fixation from our childhood, or by the actions of another person, or by a habit. Christ came to liberate us from every kind of prison until we are "free indeed" (John 8:36). God set a brain firmly on top of the human frame so that we can make sensible, loving decisions instead of being governed by animal impulses, neurotic phobias, bad habits, or the like.

"He that is slow to anger is better than the mighty; and he that ruleth his spirit than he that taketh a city" (Proverbs 16:32). Are you in control of your moods and thoughts and decisions, or are you controlled by them? Christ wants to set us free. When He is our Lord and Master, He helps us get control of ourselves, our bodies, and our lives.

4. *Patient endurance.* Patience in 2 Peter 1:6 means steadfastly keeping on, refusing to quit. In the game of life, we must not drop the ball—and if we do, we need to just pick it up and keep on playing. Jesus promised, "He who endures to the end will be saved" (Matthew 24:13 RSV). God will grant eternal life to those "who by patient continuance in well doing, seek for glory and honor and immortality" (Romans 2:7).

So, "let us run with patience the race that is set before us, looking unto Jesus the author and finisher of our faith" (Hebrews 12:1–2).

5. *Godliness.* This is another important quality to add to our faith. Godliness means becoming like God in spirit, looking at everyone with the loving attitude of the heavenly Father who "maketh his sun to rise on the evil and on the good, and sendeth rain on the just and on the unjust" (Matthew 5:45).

Godliness also means godly piety, reverencing God while at the same time treating other people justly and lovingly. The Greek historian Xenophon wrote that Socrates was "so pious and devoutly religious that he would take no step apart from the will of heaven; so just and upright that he never did even a trifling injury to any living soul." How fine it would be if that could be said about everyone who reads this book. It can, if each of us learns these secrets of abundant blessing.

6. *Brotherly kindness* (2 Peter 1:7). Jesus treated everyone like a dearly treasured sister or brother. And we must do likewise.

Abraham Lincoln was criticized during the Civil War by a woman who thought he was treating his enemies too gently. She said hotly, "We must destroy our enemies, not make them our friends!"

"Madam," the president asked, "do I not destroy my enemy when I make him my friend?"

That is the marvel of a kindly spirit. In ancient times it was said, "Love your friends and hate your enemies." Jesus said, "Love your enemies" (Matthew 5:43–44). No matter how much hatred and evil exist, brotherly love is stronger, and love will win.

7. *Love.* In this list of the things to add to our faith, the climax is love itself. Peter's word for it is *agape*, the other-directed, self-giving love that characterized Jesus. For a description of what this love is like, read the thirteenth chapter of 1 Corinthians.

Real love is more than brotherly kindness. Agape love is as broad as the love with which God loves the whole world. It is centering our whole heart and being on God, learning to love Him, and then loving everyone else the same way Jesus did.

Love is not a passive sentiment or a passing emotion. Love is action, giving ourselves like Jesus. He promised, "By this shall all men know that ye are my disciples, if ye have love one to another" (John 13:35).

As you add excellence, knowledge, self-control, steadfastness, godliness, brotherly kindness, and love to your faith, God's blessings will abound in your life.

Divine Multiplication

At one of our prayer services at the Peale Center for Christian Living, a staff member gave an illustrated talk about spiritual arithmetic. With chalk he drew a short straight line and said, "This minus sign is negative. It is flat, horizontal, limited to this material world.

"But put a line pointing upward through the middle," he continued, "and you have a plus sign. Add the spiritual world of new possibilities to your negatives, and you get pluses!"

Then the speaker said, "Now give that plus sign a shove, and you get a multiplier. What a difference! Ten plus ten becomes twenty, but ten times ten becomes a hundred!"

Is there a lesson here in spiritual arithmetic for you? Have you put a spiritual pointer into your life to turn your negatives into positives? The next time life gives you a shove, consider that maybe you are meant to move on from negativism to mere addition to the mighty power of multiplication and more abundant living.

In 2 Peter 1:8 we find some clues about rising to this super-positive level. If qualities such as goodness and brotherly love are not only within us but *abound* (or are multiplied), we are promised that we will never be "barren nor unfruitful." Instead, "an entrance shall be ministered unto you abundantly into the everlasting kingdom of our Lord and Savior Jesus Christ" (verse 11).

Principles of Prosperity

The first Psalm, like the Sermon on the Mount, and indeed the whole Bible, presents two basic ways of life. One way is lawless and "scornful"—cynical, pessimistic, completely negative. The opposite way is principled and happy, delighting in the Lord and His truth. The person who enjoys this second life-style is like a tree planted near a steadily flowing stream, its roots always supplied with life-giving water. In due season the tree brings forth fruit. Its leaves do not wither when a dry season comes because its roots go deep. Such a person "shall prosper" (verses 1–3).

The next three verses contrast "the ungodly," the person who leaves God and hope out of his life. He or she is like the chaff blown away by the wind. Nothing in such a person's life lasts because there is no staying power, nothing truly satisfying or worthwhile.

Good people have their troubles—there is no doubt about that. But by and large they have their reward too.

This first Psalm tells us how to secure God's wonderful blessings. Simply refuse to dwell in the company of godless people. Do not settle for their way of life. Do not "walk" in their counsel. Do not join the cynical and scornful. Instead, the happy and successful person delights in the laws and principles of the Lord. He learns to love God's ways and meditates on them "day and night."

Consider God's promises in Deuteronomy 28:2–12. Just before they entered the Promised Land, God promised His people every kind of blessing if they would obey Him.

He will bless you wherever you are, in the city or country (verse 3). He will bless your children and all you have (verses 4 and 5). Wherever you go, He will bless your coming and going (verse 6). Whatever you do—within His loving will—His blessings will be yours (verse 8); "The Lord shall open unto thee his good treasure" (verse 12).

> **When you center your mind on God and on His truth and abundance, good things will flow toward you rather than away from you.**

The Bible assures us that health and prosperity will be ours when our souls are in harmony with God. "I wish above all things," we read in 3 John 2, "that thou mayest prosper and be in health, even as thy soul prospereth."

When you center your mind on God and on His truth and abundance, good things will flow toward you rather than away from you. Your efforts, as you commit them to God, will be blessed, and His bountiful prosperity will encircle you. For you will be living by God's law of supply.

Practice Abundant Thinking

Again and again the Bible counsels us not to worry, fret, or be anxious about the future (Psalm 37:1; Matthew 6:25–34; 1 Peter 5:7). The fact is that the more you worry, the less likely you are to receive blessings. Worry blocks off creative thinking, shrivels accomplishment, and tends to stop the flow of prosperity.

A man I knew had a business that should have succeeded very well. But he was limited by fear and anxiety. He was afraid to make changes in his business, afraid to try new ideas and improvements, afraid to add to his rather limited inventory.

Then something happened that seemed at the time like a disaster. A competitor in the same line of business came into the community with progressive ideas and outgoing interests. His place was up-to-date and attractive, and people flocked there. The first businessman, bewildered and afraid of ruin, confessed to his pastor that he was sure he would soon be in financial shambles.

The pastor knew that this man's fear and negativism had closed off his sources of supply. He taught him real faith—in God and in himself. As a result, the businessman stopped worrying about himself and his own small interests. He overcame his fears and began thinking how he could help people in his community. As a result, customers began coming to him and, in spite of the competition, prosperity flowed his way.

Be careful what you think. Thinking scarcity and lack produces scarcity and lack. Seeking the good of others, looking for a need you can fill, and visualizing abundance creates good for yourself and those around you.

The Law of Giving

Successful living requires generous giving. The Bible promises over and over that if we give, we will receive back in abundance. Jesus said, "Give, and it shall be given unto you; good measure, pressed down, and shaken together, and running over, shall men give into your bosom. For with the same measure that ye mete [measure] withal it shall be measured to you again" (Luke 6:38).

What we give we get back. Give out hostility and anger and suspicion, and people will begin to have those feelings about you. Practice friendliness and openness, and most people will be friendly and open in return.

But there is an element of abundance in this matter of giving. When you plant one seed, normally many will be produced. One watermelon seed may produce hundreds! Jesus promised that we get back not just what we give but much more. *Good* measure, not scanty measure, will be yours. The picture in Luke 6:38 is of a merchant pressing the produce down to get more into your basket, shaking it for the same purpose, then pouring in more until your basket is running over. That is the abundant return God wants you to have.

Soon after Ruth and I were married, the Great Depression began affecting our church. The income slowed down to a trickle. The treasurer confessed that he didn't have the money to pay the preacher's salary.

Ruth and I talked together about this worrisome situation. The worries, I admit, were mostly mine. (I had not yet learned how to live very positively.) Then the two of us made a joint decision to rededicate our lives to the Lord and to trust Him with our financial affairs.

Ruth said, "Now we will take a tenth of what we have and put it into the offering next Sunday."

I said, "Let's not carry this too far! How can we do that when we're already having trouble making ends meet?"

Ruth said, "That's where we trust Him."

Reluctantly I agreed to try what the Bible calls tithing. Up to this point I had felt I was giving liberally to the Lord's work, but I had not been a complete 10 percent tither. So for me, it was quite a leap of faith.

Strangely enough, we got by. We found that the more we gave, the more the Lord gave back to us. Our decision, made so many years ago, has been followed by so many tangible blessings that now we give considerably more than the tithe.

Many have had similar experiences. R. G. LeTourneau, the great inventor of earth-moving equipment, found that he was so blessed by tithing that he kept increasing his giving until he was giving the Lord 90 percent of his income.

The Miracle of Ten Percent

The principle of tithing runs through the Bible like a gold cord. It is part of the Lord's law (Leviticus 27:30–33). Abraham and Jacob gave tithes even before the law was given (Genesis 28:22; Hebrews 7:1–6). Jesus looked with sorrow on those who tithed even the herbs from their gardens, while they neglected "the weightier matters of the law" such as justice, mercy, and faith. But he said, "These [things such as justice and faith] ought ye to have done, and not to leave the other [tithing] undone" (Matthew 23:23). In other words, He wants us to practice faith, love, and justice but to tithe also.

One of the clearest promises about prosperity is in the last book of the Old Testament. The prophet Malachi asked in amazement,

"Will a man rob God?" (Malachi 3:8). Robbery is by universal agreement an intolerable crime. Here God says that His people are robbing Him. "How have we robbed You?" the people asked. God's answer: "In tithes and offerings."

But God's complaint is followed by His amazing promise:

Bring ye all the tithes into the storehouse,
that there may be meat in mine house, and prove me now herewith, saith the Lord of hosts,
if I will not open you the windows of heaven, and pour out a blessing, that there shall not be room enough to receive it.

Malachi 3:10

Think of it! The Lord God who created this stupendous universe is telling you to prove His reality! Prove that He is alive and armed with wonder-working power by giving Him a tenth of what you get.

Thousands of people have substantiated that proof for hundreds of years by tithing. Invariably they report that when they faithfully give God 10 percent, amazing blessings pour in.

Lane Adams was working in Louisville, Kentucky, when he heard a sermon that made him furious. Lane, just starting out in the entertainment business, went to church with his wife, Annette, on a layman's Sunday. The layman who preached that day was a dentist, and his topic was tithing.

The dentist proclaimed that everyone should give one-tenth of his money to God, adding the seemingly absurd statement that a person could live well on the remaining nine-tenths. Lane said to himself, *It's not right for a guy to get up there and lie between his teeth.* He was especially upset that Annette seemed to be absorbing all this "nonsense." So as soon as church was over, he started talking a blue streak, because he was afraid she was going to talk about tithing.

As soon as Lane stopped to catch his breath, Annette said, "Honey, I think we ought to start tithing."

Fuming, Lane explained that they were in debt, they couldn't live on any less, and so on. When he stopped again to catch his breath, Annette said, "But the dentist said our first debt is to God." Then Lane said, "Okay, when our ship comes in and we have some money to do it, we'll start tithing." Annette replied, "But the dentist said that if we put God first He would provide all these things we need."

Lane got so angry at the way this dentist had hoodwinked his wife that he could hardly contain himself, but he finally agreed to try tithing, "knowing" all the time it wouldn't work. He and Annette got out all the money they had and set aside a tenth. Then they divided it between them and Lane reluctantly mailed his half of the tithe back to his home church while Annette sent her half to hers.

Incredible blessings followed. Every time Lane got a new opportunity in his business, or more money, Annette reminded him that the dentist had said wonderful things like that would happen! And they have been happening to the Adamses ever since. In his article "But the Dentist Said . . . !" in *Plus: The Magazine of Positive Thinking,* Lane wrote that after he began tithing, Jesus Christ walked off the pages of the Bible into his life, a personal, wonder-working Friend.[1]

Make your own test of God's reality. Practice the principles of abundance, and move up to a new dimension of satisfied living.

Abundance for You

God created us for abundant living. I believe that means spiritually, intellectually, emotionally, physically, and financially.

John Wesley proclaimed God's life-changing love with such power in eighteenth-century England that multitudes of men and women were able to rise to new levels of happiness and well-being. When these converts rose from degradation and misery to self-confidence and useful employment, Wesley counseled: "Get all you can, save all you can, give all you can."

I believe that is still good advice. Earn all you can from honest hard work. Save something regularly. And give generously. This will keep the abundance flowing.

Once as I was talking with John Sherrill, one of *Guideposts'* contributing editors, he asked me, "Norman, do you know how this word *abundance* originated?"

I had to admit I didn't. So John, with excitement mounting in his voice, read to me from the dictionary. He said, "Abundance comes from a Latin word that means 'to rise up in waves' or 'to overflow.'"

A picture came to me of the abundant life God wants for every one of us. His blessings come surging in like the waves of the ocean, one after the other, until we say with the psalmist, "My cup runneth over" (Psalm 23:5). We read in John 1:16, "And of his fullness have all we received, and grace for grace." Out of the riches of the presence of Jesus Christ we receive one gift of grace on top of another, like the waves tumbling in and never ceasing.

This applies to every aspect of life. The statement "Whatsoever a man soweth, that shall he also reap" (Galatians 6:7) is true literally, as everyone knows who has planted a garden. It is true spiritually: What we put into our minds and hearts will produce a harvest of either good or evil. It is also true materially, for what we invest will either bring a good return or a poor one, or, if we are careless, may be lost entirely. But if we invest in the best, with a positive attitude, we may reap dividends multiplied thirty, sixty, or many more times.

Six Ways to Handle a Problem

On a plane ride I sat next to a man who looked at me and said, "I know who you are. I've read a couple of your books. And, believe it or not, I got something out of your stuff."

I told him I was glad it had helped. Then he told me he was a traveling supervisor and that he spent a lot of time listening to the problems of employees and advising them how to be more efficient and productive.

"I have my own problems, too," he said. "In your books you stress studying the Bible and I came up with some real answers from it. In fact, I worked out six practical points for handling a problem. And they sure get results. Would you like to know what they are?"

"I certainly would!"

This is the six-point formula he gave me:

1. When faced with a problem, pray about it, asking that God's will, rather than your own, be done.
2. Having prayed, believe that God will bring the matter out right.

3. Write the problem out in detail. This gives you a clearer view of it and prevents mental confusion.
4. Always ask yourself what is the right thing to do. Nothing that is wrong ever works out right. And ask yourself if you are being fair to everyone concerned.
5. Keep working at the problem and keep thinking. Try first one thing, then another, until you find a solution.
6. When your problem is solved, thank God. Give one-tenth of your income to God's work. This is extremely important, for unless you give, the flow of God's blessings will be cut off.

I told my new friend that I thought his formula could help anyone solve the problem of "lack." This is an abundant universe, and the abundance is meant for us. God does not intend His children to subsist on a mere trickle of His goodness. He wants us to have the material means essential for normal Christian living.

To enjoy God's golden opportunities:

1. Ask yourself: Are your blessings meager or abundant?
2. Make a conscientious attempt to remove from your life everything dubious or negative. Become totally positive.
3. If life gives you a shove, become a multiplier and a sharer of God's gifts to you. What you give you will get back, with interest.
4. Decide whether you want to adopt a cynical, downbeat lifestyle or live in faith-filled abundance.
5. Refuse to think lack. Fill your mind with the thought of God's supply for every need.
6. Substitute positive expectation for negative thoughts.
7. Give God His share, and let Him multiply your blessings.
8. Above all, accept Him as your trusted Friend.

$\mathscr{A}$ Sure Cure for Fear and Stress

10

$\mathscr{B}$eing alive means having problems. How we deal with those problems can produce either misery and illness or health and happiness. And the Bible shows us how to meet our problems successfully, without fear or undue stress, even if worse comes to worst.

Four young people recently faced—and mastered—a situation so desperate that they could have lost their lives. These two young couples had been water-skiing in the middle of Long Island Sound and were on their way back toward shore, late in the afternoon, when their motorboat began losing speed. Water started welling up around the motor. They bailed it out with a potato chip bag, but the water surged in again, and then the motor began overheating.

Suddenly the boat started to sink. Grabbing life jackets, the four young people jumped into the cold water. With their marine radio they just managed to call the Coast Guard before the radio went dead. The sun dropped low in the sky.

Cheered when a helicopter approached, they watched it disappear without spotting them in the growing darkness. Their hopes rose again when several boats came near—but these too failed to find them. Julianne, especially susceptible to cold, shivered uncontrollably, and Ed's legs began to cramp. As night deepened, Angela was stung by a jellyfish. Dave encouraged Julianne to fight the cold by moving her fingers and toes and urged everyone to swim toward land. But unsure where land was in the darkness, the two couples became separated. Alone in the middle of vast Long Island Sound, what hope did they have of surviving?

About 3:30 in the morning Julianne was overcome by fatigue; her head sank into the water. Dave shook her until she revived and they kept swimming. Just before dawn broke a Coast Guard boat rescued them. Hours later, Ed and Angela managed to swim to shore.

What kept these young people from drowning during their long night in the frigid ocean? According to the article in *Northeast* magazine where I read their story, they made use of all the resources they had. They used their heads. They refused to give in to disaster. And they had faith and a positive outlook.

Dave said he "just knew" they could stay afloat. Ed said of Angela, the youngest of the four, "She was a rock. She was always positive." Angela said, "I had a lot of faith that we were going to make it. I said the Lord's Prayer at least a thousand times."

These young people have benefited from their ordeal by growing mentally and spiritually. Angela, *Northeast* magazine reports, no longer gives in to the stress of schoolwork and deadlines. Every night before she goes to bed, she says, "I look back at the day and pick out the good points." From triumphing over that near disaster by drawing on a power greater than themselves, the four young people have acquired the confidence that they can make it through any crisis.[1]

For valuable counsel in overcoming stress when a situation looks hopeless, please look with me at another true story of a close call at sea. You will find it in the Bible in Acts 27.

Arrested for witnessing to his faith, Paul was sent on a long sea voyage to Rome, where he was to be tried before the emperor. Facing tempestuous autumn winds, the vessel raced past the Mediterranean islands of Cyprus and Crete and then was caught in a fierce gale. For fourteen days the storm was so violent that neither sun nor stars (the only means of navigating) could be seen through the spray-drenched darkness. Finally every human hope of surviving came to an end (verse 20).

Worse still, as the ship finally approached land, the sailors made ready to escape in the only lifeboat, abandoning the passengers to certain death.

But there was one man among the 276 passengers who knew what to do. Paul, the prisoner, took command; he made known what the sailors were doing and halted their exodus. Then he explained how everyone on board could be saved, and by following his advice all 276 survived that frightening ordeal.

Eight Keys to a Good Outcome of Your Crisis

When disaster strikes, there is always hope if we keep calm and think. Let's examine how Paul averted the impending calamity, for in our own crisis we can follow the same steps to a successful outcome.

1. *Take charge.* The story of Paul's voyage to Italy fills only one chapter of the Bible, but the voyage itself took many weeks. Paul knew from his sea travels that being in the Mediterranean during the rough weather of autumn could be difficult and dangerous. He could have told himself that he was a helpless prisoner and done nothing. But Paul was a take-charge individual. He warned of the dangers ahead (Acts 27:9–10).

God does not want us to be timid, shrinking violets. He gives each of us the responsibility and the power to take charge of our lives and to do what needs to be done.

Dr. S. I. McMillen, a physician and medical missionary, wrote a valuable book called *None of These Diseases* suggesting four ways we can take control of a stressful situation: (1) Diversify the stressful agents by creating variety in your life. (2) Avoid long exposure to stress whenever possible. Over one fourth of one group of men who had heart attacks had been working more than seventy hours a week. Learn to relax. (3) Don't overextend yourself. Concentrate instead on what you do well. (4) Take a positive attitude toward what you do. Don't let anger destroy you. Dr. McMillen revealed that at one time he nearly died of a bleeding ulcer because of a faulty reaction to a minor incident. He decided he had generated ten dollars' worth of dangerous adrenaline over something worth only ten cents![2]

2. *Be an encourager.* Although Paul's warning was ignored, events proved him right. On leaving Crete, the ship was caught in a wind like a hurricane; the only choice was to lower the sails and go with the storm. The winds hurled the ship through the waves with such violence that everyone else lost hope of surviving. For many days, no one could even eat.

At that desperate point, Paul again took charge. Gathering the passengers around, he urged everyone to "be of good cheer," assuring them that no life would be lost (verse 22).

God constantly encourages us (Isaiah 41:10; 2 Corinthians 1:4). When we encourage others we fill our own hearts with courage and strength.

3. *Remember whose you are.* Paul knew to whom he belonged (Acts 27:23). And the God to whom he had committed himself stood by him in every crisis.

The Book of Daniel tells of one of the worst disasters imaginable. When three young men, Shadrach, Meshach, and Abednego, refused to worship the ninety-foot golden idol set up by King Nebuchadnezzar, the king had them thrown into a furnace so hot that its flames killed the men who cast them in (Daniel 3:1–22).

But when the king came to see the charred remains of the three faithful men, he found an incredible sight. The three were walking in the midst of the fire—and with them walked a fourth, one "like the Son of God" (verse 25). Still today, those who have the courage of their convictions and do what is right regardless of the consequences may pass through "fiery furnaces," but they will find themselves supported and protected by a Power greater than themselves.

Life is full of fiery furnaces. A high-school student faces the heat of being called a sissy if he doesn't take drugs. A businessperson may go through the furnace of contempt from some of his associates if he takes a stand for the right way instead of the easy way. A hostess may hesitate to invite a poor family to dinner for fear of what the neighbors might say. Sooner or later all of us face such situations. But God will always stand by and reward those who refuse to worship false idols.

4. *Say good-bye to fear.* God sent an angelic messenger to Paul with the words "Fear not" (Acts 27:24). In a crisis the worst thing we can do is to give in to fear. The Bible acknowledges that fear often disturbs our lives, so again and again God tells us not to fear. For just a few examples of this look at Deuteronomy 1:21; 1 Chronicles 28:20; Isaiah 35:4; Matthew 10:31; 2 Timothy 1:7; and Revelation 2:10. Let faith put an end to fear.

5. *Trust God.* Paul knew he could be secure because he believed (verse 25). The great poet John Greenleaf Whittier was conscious of the things that were wrong in his world, but he wrote in faith:

> Yet, in the maddening maze of things,
>   And tossed by storm and flood,
> To one fixed trust my spirit clings:
>   I know that God is good![3]

6. *Do all you can for a good outcome.* Faith does not mean doing nothing. On the contrary, true faith means being ready to do what God shows us we can do. When Paul saw the sailors beginning to jump ship, he warned the centurion in charge, "Unless these men stay with us, we cannot hope to survive" (verse 31).

When you do your best, God adds His best, and miracles can happen.

7. *Be practical.* Paul was aware that during the two weeks of storm and stress, no one ate anything. Setting the example, he broke a loaf of bread and passed it around, urging everyone to eat in order to gain strength for the tasks ahead (verses 33–35).

It has been said that Christianity is the most practical religion. While other faiths often renounce physical things, the Bible shows us how to live at our best in this everyday world. The whole book of Proverbs emphasizes this, and the Gospels and Epistles give counsel about the importance of faithful work, the dangers of overindulgence, laziness, and other negativisms, and the practical ways to good relationships.

8. *Be thankful.* Paul gave thanks when he ate (verse 35). He thanked God again when he found new spiritual brothers (Acts 28:15). In fact, the apostle made a habit of giving thanks (Romans

1:8; 1 Corinthians 1:4). The attitude of gratitude is one of the vital steps to happy, healthy, successful, positive living.

As you practice these principles you will find that you can face whatever comes your way with equanimity and go forward to victory.

Fear and Anxiety Today

Many people find themselves caught in the grip of abysmal fear and stress. Some worry about losing a job. Others, unemployed, have to deal with the stress this causes. There are those who fear the cost and chaos of dealing with an illness. Others worry about balancing living costs and income. Many are concerned about the ill health of friends or loved ones, about someone's addiction to a bad habit, or other serious problems.

Such things can be very distressing. But it is important to find a way to deal with distress, because worse than any problem are the fear and anxiety that paralyze us and prevent constructive solutions.

Dr. Dean Ornish, a specialist in internal medicine who wrote the book *Reversing Heart Disease,* said in a recent interview: "Stress comes not from what you do but from how you react to what you do." In other words, never underestimate the power of a positive attitude.

My friend Charles L. Allen once received a telephone call from a woman who told him she was ill and that she would probably not live long. She begged him to help her die with a clear conscience.

This was her story: More than forty years earlier, while at work, she had taken ten dollars from the cash register. Now she wanted to right the wrong by returning the money, but she was apparently afraid to do it herself. So she asked Dr. Allen if she could send the money to him and if he would return it for her. He told her he would help her, but he wondered why she had not returned the money long before, saving herself all those years of anxiety!

All of us collect a lot of mental baggage over the years. If there is anything wrong in your past, make it right as far as that is possible. Then ask your Savior to forgive it. To anyone who asks His forgiveness, the Lord promises, "I am he that blotteth out thy transgressions for mine own sake, and will not remember thy sins" (Isaiah 43:25). God forgives and forgets. Let us do likewise. After you have confessed your sins, refuse to think about them any more.

I have often thought that worry is true to its name. It derives from an old Anglo-Saxon word, *wyrgan*, that means to choke or strangle—and it does exactly that. Worry chokes our hopes and strangles our spirits, draining our very life.

Worry and fear can trigger illnesses. When a person faces a crisis, too much work, or almost any kind of change, his brain releases adrenaline and other chemicals into his system, temporarily stopping digestion and increasing blood pressure, blood sugar, and pulse rate. These prepare the whole body for heroic action.

While I was writing this book a friend wrote to me:

> I know a little about stress from my own experience. Years ago when my children were small, I was working for a religious publisher in New Jersey. One day my wife had our car and I was waiting in our office for her to arrive so I could go home at the end of the day. I remember standing at my office window looking for her when there was a sudden noise behind me. Our three smallest children had crept quietly into the building and decided to surprise their daddy by shouting "SURPRISE!" as they rushed into my office.
>
> The children were very good at making a noiseless entrance. I had no idea they were there until they charged in, shouting. I remember my instant reaction: I jumped, making a complete semicircle before I landed, to face this unknown danger! I imagine a lot of adrenaline charged into my system at that moment!

That is exactly how stress works. God has put within our bodies this marvelous mechanism that prepares us for "fight or flight" when danger threatens. It is the same mechanism that enables a sleeping deer, when it senses danger, to bound into the air, its legs pumping, ready for instant flight.

But the same chemicals that prepare us for a crisis can have a poisonous effect unless we react positively. They can cause indigestion, ulcers, headaches, backaches, neck pains, depression, high blood pressure, heart attacks, and other problems.

No wonder the Book of Ecclesiastes says, "Remove vexation from your mind, and put away pain from your body" (11:10 RSV) and Proverbs warns of the dangers of anxiety: "Heaviness in the heart of man maketh it stoop" (12:25).

Jesus, of course, speaks clearly of the dangers of worrying (Matthew 6:25–34). And Philippians tells us to have no anxiety about anything (4:6).

The Good News about Fear and Worry

I am aware of the real problems so many individuals have today and how difficult it is to face such problems without worrying. The good news of the Bible is that we *can* meet them without succumbing to fear or worry! And the Scriptures show us how to do it.

We can learn much about handling worry and fear from the fourteenth chapter of John. The Savior has gathered His disciples together for the last time before the crucifixion. He knows their hearts are troubled at the prospect of His imminent death, so He tells them not to let that anxiety continue. For a troubled heart spells trouble. Yet how can they stop worrying? The first thing they (and we) must learn is to "believe in God, believe also in me" (verse 1).

Believe! Trust your loving, caring heavenly Father. He has a purpose in letting you experience this problem you are facing. He will see you through it. And put your faith in Jesus, who has experienced every kind of problem we can have (Hebrews 4:15). He was tempted and tested and harassed just as we sometimes are. He knows from His life on earth how hard it is to meet turmoil, stress, and opposition. But He solved His problems, and He will help you solve yours.

Accept His Peace

The same fourteenth chapter of John shows, in verse 27, how to overcome anxiety and fear:

> Peace I leave with you, my peace I give unto you: not as the world giveth, give I unto you. Let not your heart be troubled, neither let it be afraid.

When Jesus died, He left no money or land behind, but He did bequeath to all His followers (including you and me) the legacy of peace. It is our inheritance. We do not have to struggle for it or work for it. He *gives* it to us.

Peace means far more than the absence of conflict. That is a modern negative concept of this rich word. In the Bible the absence of war is usually called "rest" rather than peace (Joshua 14:15; Judges 5:31; 1 Chronicles 22:18). Throughout Scripture peace has a marvelous, totally positive content. The Old Testament word for it is *shalom*; this is still a popular Jewish greeting, the equivalent of the Arabs' *salaam*, basically meaning "May everything good be yours," similar to the original meaning of our "good-bye."

William Barclay writes about the meaning of peace:

It means "right relationships between man and man," true fellowship, not just polite tolerance. In Matthew 5:9 the translation should be: "O the bliss of those who make friends with each other.". . . It means "everything which makes for a man's highest good." . . . It is therefore not sufficient to translate: "Go in peace" (e.g. Mark 5:34) as even the NEB does. It is better to translate quite simply: "Go, and God bless you!"[4]

Accept Christ's gift. Say to Jesus, "Lord, thank You for this wonderful gift of peace. I accept Your gift as my inheritance. I will let Your harmony and blessing fill my heart and mind until it is troubled no more."

As you do this, think of how Jesus once fell asleep in a storm. After a strenuous day, He and His disciples were crossing the Sea of Galilee when a disastrous tempest arose (Mark 4:35–41). The wind blew so hard and the waves were so high that the boat was filled with water. All the time Jesus was asleep. The disciples must have been exasperated: "Master, carest thou not that we perish?" (verse 38). Of course He cared! Was He waiting for them to ask for help? As soon as they did, He calmed the great storm with the command, "Peace, be still" (verse 39). And He calmed the minds of the frightened men as well.

If you are anxious and troubled about something, perhaps you need, as the disciples did, to awaken the Lord asleep within you. Tell Him all about your need. Listen to Him say to you, "Peace, be still." Let His words and His healing peace quiet the storm in your heart and mind. Then you will be ready for His solution to your problem.

What Is Christ's Peace?

Jesus said, "My peace I give unto you" (John 14:27). His peace is the kind of harmony and serenity within and without that He demonstrated throughout His life: rest in God, loving good-will, and calm, confident control of every situation.

And He gives it "not as the world giveth." When Jesus speaks of the world, He is not referring to the beautiful planet God made for us, but to the wicked world system that degrades and destroys it. That evil world always promises more than it gives, while God always gives more than He promises. This world's "free" gifts all have a catch; His alone are absolutely free. The world's gifts look good but often disappoint us; His gifts are even more wonderful than we expect. The former, at best, soon diminish or wear out; the Lord's gifts continually increase in value and satisfaction.

And all that is especially true of Christ's gift of peace. It is a quietness and confidence of heart that renews our spirits and helps us live each day in harmony with God, His creation, and His children. It is deeper than human understanding (Philippians 4:7). The marvelous fact is that Christ Himself *is* our peace (Ephesians 2:14). When we trust Him, we have it all.

Calm your mind and soul with these words from an old hymn:

> Safe am I in the hollow of His hand,
> Sheltered o'er with love for evermore.
> No ill can harm me, no foe alarm me:
> For He keeps both day and night.
> Safe am I in the hollow of His hand.[5]

The Result of Christ's Peace

Two things result from Christ's gift of peace to us. The heart filled with Christ's peace can no more be troubled than a serene pond on a quiet day can be wracked with waves. Nor will it fear, for just as perfect love casts out all fear (1 John 4:18), so does Christ's perfect peace.

A very responsible lady in Texas wrote to my wife and me recently:

> When I went for a physical the doctor found a mass in one of my breasts. Since my mom died of cancer about two and a half years ago and my thirty-one-year-old nephew died of cancer two months earlier, I guess I'm a good candidate for it.
>
> So I did the best I could applying God's Word to my life. I told God I didn't want cancer; so I would empty my mind of anxiety, fear, and all insecurities. I watched those dirty things go down the drain. Then I told the Lord, "This old disease or whatever it is I have, I don't want it. Lord, here it is, I give it to You and I'm walking away and leaving it with You."
>
> I pictured the Lord taking it in His hands and going to the edge of a cliff to drop it. Then I'd fill my mind with thoughts of love, peace, joy, serenity, tranquillity, things that are beautiful, honest, of good report, and every good thing I could think of from God's Word.
>
> When I went last month for another mammogram, there was no sign of the mass—just a lot of scar tissue. I think I had a happy doctor, and I know I was very happy. Praise the Lord.

This is a wonderful example of the result of replacing worry and fear thoughts with faith, prayer, hope, love, joy, peace, and serenity. When these positive values rule our minds, there is no place for the negative emotions that lead to unhappiness, failure, and disease.

Try this experiment. Write down what you have been thinking about most in the last few hours. Have your thoughts been tinged with worry and fear, or with thankfulness and anticipation? The last time you spoke to someone, did you talk about negative things or hopeful, positive topics?

If you find you have been letting tension and anxiety control your thoughts, ask God to help you drop such thoughts and to replace them with a sense of His peace. He will.

Promises of Peace

Make the following words your own by committing them to memory and repeating them often.

> **God's promises of peace, accepted in the mind and heart and verbalized frequently, are a sure cure for tension and fear.**

Thou wilt keep him in perfect peace, whose mind is stayed on thee (Isaiah 26:3).

Come unto me, all ye that labor and are heavy laden, and I will give you rest (Matthew 11:28).

These things I have spoken unto you, that in me ye might have peace (John 20:26).

Jesus . . . said, Peace be unto you (John 20:26).

Now the God of hope fill you with all joy and peace in believing (Romans 15:13).

God's promises of peace, accepted in the mind and heart and verbalized frequently, are a sure cure for tension and fear.

Experiencing God's Peace

Try to imagine the distress Horatio Spafford, a Chicago businessman, must have felt when he learned from the newspapers that the ship carrying his family to Europe in 1873 had sunk in the Atlantic. Two weeks later a cablegram came from his wife, Anna: SAVED ALONE.

The ship had collided with another vessel near Newfoundland, sinking in twelve minutes. A falling mast stunned Anna; when she came to, she found that all four of her children had gone down with 474 other passengers. She was one of the twenty-two who survived, reaching Cardiff, Wales, after two long weeks on the crowded sailing vessel that plucked them from the icy ocean.

Horatio sailed immediately to Wales to be with his wife. When his ship reached the spot where his children had perished, he was moved to write these words:

> When peace, like a river, attendeth my way,
> when sorrows like sea billows roll;
> Whatever my lot, Thou hast taught me to say,
> It is well, it is well with my soul.[6]

Spafford's words became a hymn that has helped millions of people face the worst imaginable disasters in the peace of Christ. But that is not the end of this true story, which was researched by my associate George Hart III. Horatio and Anna gave the rest of their lives to founding and operating the American Colony and the Spafford Memorial Children's Hospital in Jerusalem, providing food, education, and hospital care for thousands of poor children and their mothers.

Deeply committed Christians, Horatio and Anna Spafford made God's peace part of their life, and they brought that peace to many others.

Verbalize, Visualize, Vitalize

God's peace is a sure cure for tension and fear. But we must make His promises of peace part of our lives.

Verbalize them: Repeat them over and over until they permeate your subconscious.

Visualize the peace of Christ: Picture His loving good will surrounding you, filling you, enveloping you in harmonious tranquillity.

Vitalize: Make peace a vital center in your life. Practice peace. Refuse to let disharmony bring you distress. Become a peacemaker in all your relationships. It is not the problems you meet but how you face them that counts. Confront the stressful situations that come your way with trusting, peace-filled confidence. Then, instead of being overwhelmed, you can make the most of life, whatever happens.

To overcome fear and anxiety:

1. Believe that you can solve whatever problems you face.
2. Never see yourself as a victim of circumstances. Take charge of your life.
3. Encourage others in their difficulties.
4. Trust the Lord to see you through.
5. Refuse to let fear or worry control you.
6. Do all you can for a good outcome of your difficulty.
7. Don't let stress from the past ruin the present.

8. Accept the blessing-packed peace God is giving you.
9. Fill your mind and heart with His promises of peace.
10. Be a true peacemaker. Let the Lord help you defuse difficult relationships, live in joyful harmony, and bring His wondrous blessings to others.
11. Verbalize, visualize, and vitalize the peace of Christ.

GOD'S WAY TO GOOD HEALTH AND LONG LIFE

*T*he Bible is both a book of spiritual wisdom and a valuable treasury of principles and prescriptions for happy, harmonious, healthful living here and now. It is filled with examples of vigorous, vital individuals. Can you imagine a sickly Adam, an invalid Eve, tubercular prophets, diseased apostles, or an ailing Jesus?

On the contrary, numerous personalities of Scripture were great examples of good health, and they often lived to an astounding age. Moses began his great work when he was eighty, and when he died forty years later (at 120!) "his eye was not dim, nor his natural force abated" (Deuteronomy 34:7). Elijah was a man of tremendous vigor; he could run many miles, faster than the horses that pulled King Ahab's chariot (1 Kings 18:44–46). Daniel and his Jewish friends who forsook King Nebuchadnezzar's handouts of wine and meat for a diet of water and vegetables were healthier, better looking, and wiser than their pagan counterparts (Daniel 1:11–15).

Jesus must have been a strong specimen of manhood. Trained as a carpenter, He had to exercise His muscles strenuously. He walked long distances, enjoyed a simple diet, mainly of bread, fish and fruit, and endured tremendous suffering at the end of His earthly life. Even after He had been beaten and crowned with thorns, Pontius Pilate, seeing Him, exclaimed, "Behold the man" (John 19:5). What a man!

The Bible is God's prescription for both spiritual and physical well-being.

Not only our Lord but such characters of the Bible as Elijah, Elisha, Isaiah, Peter, and Paul performed great miracles of healing. At the beginning of His ministry, Jesus announced that His mission was to bring sight to the blind, to free those who had been bruised, to proclaim deliverance, and to heal (Luke 4:18). Throughout the Gospels we see Him straightening crooked limbs, energizing the paralyzed, restoring the insane to mental health, and healing "all manner of diseases." Additionally, we learn from Scripture that "gifts of healings" are a continuing and important part of His work (1 Corinthians 12:28).

The Bible is God's prescription for both spiritual and physical well-being. The psalmist exulted, "The Lord is the strength of my life" (Psalm 27:1). J. B. Phillips words one of Paul's great statements about good health as follows:

"Once the Spirit of him who raised Christ Jesus from the dead lives within you he will, by that same Spirit, bring to your whole being, yes even your mortal bodies, new strength and vitality" (Romans 8:11).

Dr. S. I. McMillen's book *None of These Diseases* outlines some of the ways the Bible leads to good health.[1] For instance, when the Lord brought the Israelites out of Egypt, He promised, "If thou wilt diligently hearken to the voice of the Lord thy God, and wilt do that which is right in His sight, and wilt give ear to his commandments, and keep all his statutes, I will put none of these diseases upon thee, which I have brought upon the Egyptians: for I am the Lord that healeth thee" (Exodus 15:26).

Later on He said: "You shall walk in all the way which the Lord your God has commanded you, that you may live, and that it may go well with you, and that you may live long in the land which you shall possess" (Deuteronomy 5:33 RSV). The Proverbs promise: "Fear the Lord, and turn away from evil. It will be healing to your flesh and refreshment to your bones" (3:7–8 RSV). And we read in the Third Epistle of John: "Beloved, I wish above all things that thou mayest prosper and be in health, even as thy soul prospereth" (verse 2).

Dr. McMillen recounts the dreadful history of medicine before sanitation was discovered. During the Middle Ages millions died from such plagues as leprosy and the Black Death. There was little the medical profession could do. These plagues were finally brought under control, he notes, because the church pioneered in practicing the Bible's prescription for dealing with contagion: the quarantine (Leviticus 13:46).

Even during the time of the American Civil War, medical sanitation was practically unknown. Dr. Ignaz Semmelweis discovered that many patients examined by doctors frequently died soon afterward. Theorizing that they were transmitting diseases, Dr. Semmelweis ordered the physicians in his ward to wash their hands after examining sick or deceased individuals, whereupon most of the deaths ceased.

Dr. McMillen notes that the Mosaic laws give detailed instructions about handling the dead or diseased. They prescribe careful washing of the hands after touching the sick or deceased. If these rules had been followed in the past, countless millions of lives could have been saved.

Attitudes of Health

The Bible encourages the good attitudes that support good health. The wisest men throughout history have been aware of this relationship. Four centuries before Christ, Hippocrates, who might be called the father of medicine, taught his students to note the emotional states and the general background of their patients. He believed that health is affected by the mind, and that to be whole a person must get into harmony with himself and with the world around him.

The Bible teaches two basic principles about attitudes and health. First, positive spiritual attitudes enhance health. Attention to God's Word and His principles is given as the key to "life unto those that find them, and health to all their flesh" (Proverbs 4:22). The therapeutic effects of laughter and joy are extolled in Proverbs 17:22.

On the other hand, the Bible clearly teaches that negative thoughts and unwholesome practices can produce sickness and even death. Long before the AIDS epidemic, the Book of Proverbs taught that promiscuous sexual practices can lead to death (Proverbs 7:22–27). In the Book of Acts we read of a man and his wife who died during the stress of trying to maintain a dishonest transaction with a series of lies (Acts 5:1–11).

In modern times medical science has begun to make the connection between attitudes and health. William James, the great Harvard psychologist who has been called the father of American psychological science, believed that the mind contains deep reservoirs of healing power. Dr. William Osler, a famous physician at Johns Hopkins University Medical School, was convinced that the emotions affect migraine headaches, neurasthenia, and other ailments. He said: "The care of tuberculosis depends more on what the patient has in his head than what he has in his chest."

Dr. Tohru Ishigami, a Japanese physician who worked for ten years with victims of tuberculosis, noted the connection between his patients' emotional lives and their disease. "The personal history," he reported in *The American Review of Tuberculosis*, "usually reveals failure in business, lack of harmony in the family, or jealousy of some sort. Nervous individuals are especially prone to attacks of this type, and the prognosis is generally bad." On the other hand, wrote Dr. Ishigami, a number of patients who recovered from severe cases of tuberculosis were "optimistic and not easily worried."[2]

Strange as it may seem, however, the medical world is still somewhat divided over the relationship between the mind and health. But now there are fewer medical people who question such a relationship. There appears to be a growing consensus that the mind and emotions do mightily affect our health.

It has often been demonstrated that if psychological factors can contribute to disease, they can also lead to healing. John D. Rockefeller, Sr., at the age of fifty-three was probably the richest man on earth. But relentless pursuit of money took its toll from his health. With an income of over a million dollars a week, he lost all his hair and he could eat only crackers and milk!

But Rockefeller began using his vast wealth to benefit others. As he turned his thoughts from making money to the good that money can accomplish, Rockefeller's health improved. "He began to sleep, to eat normally, and to enjoy life in general," says Dr. McMillen, adding that "into the soul of John D. came refreshing streams of love and gratitude from those whom he was helping." The billionaire's health changed so radically that he lived until he was ninety-eight.

Dr. Bernard S. Siegel, a remarkable surgeon who teaches at Yale University, is a strong believer in the close connection between health and attitudes. Sometimes he asks a patient: "Why do you need this disease?" Once the person recognizes the dynamics of his life situation, he is able to cooperate more effectively in the healing process. Dr. Siegel uses imagery and the patient's emotions to help bring this about. In his book *Love, Medicine and Miracles* he says: "We must remove the word 'impossible' from our vocabulary. As David Ben-Gurion once observed in another context, 'Anyone who doesn't believe in miracles is not a realist.'"[3]

Among the growing number of physicians who use mental imaging in the healing process is Gerald Epstein, who treats most of his patients' physical problems by prescribing exercises in imagery. If a patient has the immune disorder of mononucleosis, for example, Dr. Epstein asks her or him to relax and to picture white knights (which could well symbolize the immune system's white blood cells) occupying a fort and pushing out an army of hostile warriors.[4] My friend Harry DeCamp used a similar mental process, utilizing this healing power which God has put within the imagination, to overcome such a severe case of cancer that he had been pronounced inoperable and given "no time" to live. (At this writing, years later, he is a radiant picture of good health.)

This process of using the mind to energize the body is clearly taught in the Bible. One woman, believing that just getting close to Jesus and touching His robe would heal her, did just that. Jesus became aware of her effort and said, "Daughter, your faith has made you well" (Mark 5:34 RSV).

Accept the Healing Power of God

No one, of course, is immune to the problems and vicissitudes of life. But if some malady attacks us, we can remember that God is the source of health and healing.

The psalmist blessed the Lord "who forgiveth all thine iniquities; who healeth all thy diseases" (Psalm 103:3). He told the Israelites,

"I am the Lord that healeth thee" (Exodus 15:26). Jesus healed "all manner of sickness" (Matthew 4:23). He told His disciples to "heal the sick" (Luke 10:9).

If sickness or an accident strikes you or a loved one, here are some suggestions for releasing the Lord's healing power.

1. *Practice the principles of wholesome thinking and living.* Never dwell on the illness. Instead, picture yourself or the person afflicted as whole and well. Remember: "For as he thinketh in his heart, so is he" (Proverbs 23:7).

2. *Pray with a positive mental attitude.* Our Lord tells us: "What things soever ye desire, when ye pray, believe that ye receive them, and ye shall have them" (Mark 11:24). Scholars tell me that the original Greek here is even stronger and is better translated as the New English Bible puts it: "Whatever you ask for in prayer, believe that you have received it and it will be yours."

Yes, believe that you have received what you ask, and it will be yours. Try your hardest to believe that the Lord will answer your prayer. With your inner eye see the person you are praying for whole and well. Hold that vision in your heart.

I always pray for the healing of hospital patients, even if the doctor says there is no hope. God's answer is not always to heal them in this life, but our responsibility is to always be open to the possibility of the flow of His power.

3. *Remember that God made your body for health and wholeness.* The distinguished physician Lewis Thomas says that the human body is the most wonderful thing in this whole wonderful universe, and that we ought to celebrate this "absolute marvel of good health" instead of concentrating so much on the possibility of illness. He writes in *A Long Line of Cells:* "We are paying too little attention, and respect, to the built-in durability and power of the human organism. Its surest tendency is toward stability and balance."[5] God has put amazing healing powers within our bodies and minds. As a result, it could almost be said that the body heals itself.

4. *Keep your mind filled with the great life-affirming principles and promises of the Bible.* When he was twenty-eight years old, William James had a severe emotional breakdown. He was obsessed with fear that he might be committed to an asylum—and in his day,

lunatic asylums were often horrors. He said his despondency and fear were so invasive and powerful that, "if I had not clung to Scripture texts like 'The eternal God is my refuge' [and] 'I am the resurrection and the life,' etc., I think I should have grown really insane."[6]

Look up and think up! Memorize and repeat some of these great verses:

> I am the Lord that healeth thee (Exodus 15:26).
> He healeth the broken in heart, and bindeth up their wounds (Psalm 147:3).
> He was wounded for our transgressions, he was bruised for our iniquities: the chastisement of our peace was upon him; and with his stripes we are healed (Isaiah 53:5).
> Unto you that fear my name shall the Sun of righteousness arise with healing in his wings (Malachi 4:2).
> The prayer of faith shall save the sick (James 5:15).
> Confess your faults one to another, and pray for one another, that ye may be healed (James 5:16).
> By whose stripes ye were healed (1 Peter 2:24).
> Jesus Christ maketh thee whole (Acts 9:34).

As God's truth fills your mind and heart and life, you will experience His healing presence and power. A natural result, amazing to many people, is the actual lengthening of life.

Never Grow Old

If we truly believe and practice the teachings of Scripture, we may advance in years but we will never really grow old. We will say with David that the Lord "satisfieth thy mouth with good things; so that thy youth is renewed like the eagle's" (Psalm 103:5).

Although most birds live only a few years, some eagles have been known to live more than fifty years. Did you ever hear of an old, doddering, senile eagle? I haven't. Eagles live majestically throughout their lives, and so can we.

When we live as God intends us to, we can say with Paul:

> Even if the physical part of us inevitably deteriorates, spiritually we are renewed every day. We have our troubles, but they are tran-

sitory and unimportant, and all the time they are producing for us a superlative and eternal glory, which will far outweigh all the troubles.

2 Corinthians 4:16–17 Barclay

With God's Word in your mind, you can stay young all your life. All you need to do is to think young, and believe. For life is the gift of God, and Jesus came to bring us life in all its fullness (John 10:10).

A few years ago I clipped out of the newspaper a story about James A. Hard, who lived to the age of 111. One way this man cooperated with the forces of health was to take everything in stride. He never let himself get overly excited or upset about things. His friends said he was always happy.

When he was ninety, James Hard had a cataract on one eye. His granddaughter told the story: "We were going to arrange the operation in a hospital, but Grandpa beat us to it. All by himself, he went to the physician's office where the doctor performed the operation. After the required resting period, he came home by himself in a cab. That is having grit and courage."

Emotional tranquillity, refusal to worry, the attitude of happiness, zest for life, grit, and courage—these all bring about better health and longer life, so that our youth, too, is "renewed like the eagle's."

Long life is God's promise to those who:

- Turn away from evil (Psalm 34:11–14)
- Obey the Lord (Proverbs 3:1–2)
- Revere and honor Him (Psalm 128:1, 6)
- Honor their parents (Ephesians 6:2–3)

Psalm 92:12 tells us that the "righteous"—Scripture's description of those who trust God and walk in His ways—will flourish like majestic cedar trees or life-maintaining palm trees. And "They shall still bring forth fruit in old age" (verse 14). That is a wonderful promise. All the great values of human character continue and develop as the years pass. No doubt this was the reason that spiritual leadership in Bible times was put into the hands of "elders" who were mature spiritually and mentally as well as physically.

What kind of life span can we expect? According to Genesis 6:3, people in ancient times could expect to live 120 years. Dr. Roy L Walford, professor of pathology at the UCLA School of Medicine, has written a book entitled *The 120 Year Diet* in which he says it is possible for a person to enjoy exactly that many years with a sensible life-style and a low-calorie, high-nutrition diet. And Dr. Ben H. Douglas points out that scientists have extended the life span of several different species of animals by 30 to 40 percent through a restricted diet. A similar extension of the human life span, he writes in his book *AgeLess*, "would mean that humans could live to be 140 to 150 years old." He adds that exercise, good nutrition, and positive attitudes produce happier and healthier years as well as more of them.[7] Dr. Linus Pauling, twice a Nobel Prize recipient, estimates that proper health measures could increase one's life span by twenty-five to thirty-five years.[8]

Yes, you can be happy and productive for many years. Claim the Lord's promise in Psalm 92:14: "They shall still bring forth fruit in old age." Write out the words of that promise, put them where you can see them, and grow young along with me!

Look Forward to Your Golden Years

Unfortunately, the final years of life are sometimes spoken of disparagingly. Never speak or think that way. Listen to Andrew G. Goliszek, a research scientist with the Department of Biology of North Carolina A & T University: "At the present time, there's no evidence at all that aging produces a change in intelligence, learning capacity, memory, or information processing. In fact, while some special skills aren't performed so successfully after forty, intellectual functions that rely on the application of learned material remain intact well into our seventies."[9]

The fact is that Browning's poetic line "The best is yet to be" is scientifically valid. Your later years can be increasingly blessed and helpful to others.

Today more than thirty million Americans are over sixty-five, and the number is steadily increasing. Furthermore, there are great numbers of men and women in their seventies, eighties, and nineties who are doing valuable work. When literacy expert Frank

Laubach and missionary statesman E. Stanley Jones were forced to retire from their work officially, both men went right on working, unofficially, in their respective callings for many more years. Dr. Jones wrote when he was eighty-three: "I have been speaking from two to five times a day for fifty years and taking no vacation except to write a book. I find my hand is steady, my body sound, and there is no weariness or exhaustion—none that a good night's rest will not throw off."[10]

Here are some Bible-based suggestions for enjoying truly golden years.

1. *Expect a good old age.* Whatever anyone "thinketh in his heart, so is he" (Proverbs 23:7). If you expect life to go from bad to worse, it probably will. But if you determine to make your life a blessing for others, if you take time to enjoy the wonderful world God has given us, if you look for the good in each day and look forward with thankfulness, and if you anticipate God's constant guidance and care, you will find life richly rewarding.

I am told of a widow in New Jersey, now in her eighties, who is intensely interested in nature and other subjects. Among her numerous hobbies, she studies the stars with her own powerful telescope. Her favorite television program is my friend Robert Schuller's Hour of Power. This lady has so many interests that she said recently to one of my associates, "I don't know if I'll be able to do all that I want to do before this century ends." Such a positive, forward-looking attitude almost guarantees good health and long life.

2. *Live sensibly, as the Bible cautions us.* The Book of Proverbs provides numerous admonitions for successful everyday living, including healthful living. Chapters 5 and 7 detail some of the dangers of sexual immorality. Put the words of Proverbs 7:22–23 together with the alarming increase today in illnesses and deaths from sexually transmitted diseases, and ask yourself which is the more sensible: the Bible or "the new morality"?

Proverbs 23:21 and many other passages warn against the dangers of intemperate eating and drinking. But the Bible also suggests moderation even in fasting. When 276 passengers had gone without food for two weeks during a disastrous storm in the Mediterranean, Paul wisely advised them to eat, saying "for this is for your health" (Acts 27:34).

In a pamphlet published by Blue Cross and Blue Shield, based on a study by Nedra Belloc and Dr. Lester Breslow, the advice is given, "Don't junk your body too soon." The study indicates that the average individual can expect eleven extra years of life by following these seven simple rules:

1. Eat breakfast regularly.
2. Eat three square meals a day.
3. Get seven to eight hours of sleep every day.
4. Exercise moderately two or three times a week.
5. Keep your weight normal.
6. Drink moderately or not at all.
7. Don't smoke cigarettes.

All this is entirely consistent with the wise counsel and the examples of the Bible.

Noel Johnson is a Californian over ninety years old who runs in marathons. But he was not always healthy. During his sixties, in fact, Johnson was in such bad shape that his doctor told him any physical activity might be fatal. He was forty pounds overweight and plagued with high blood pressure, arthritis, and bursitis.

When his son wanted to put him into a nursing home, Noel Johnson came to his senses. Studying the principles of good health and long life, he determined to change his ways. He started exercising and running. By the age of seventy-one he was running the mile in six and a half minutes, and he had won three gold medals. In 1989, 1990, and 1991 he was one of several ninety-year-olds who ran in the grueling New York Marathon.

Noel Johnson says he has discovered "the fountain of youth" through exercise, good diet, and positive thinking. "I'm trying to get the word out," he told an interviewer recently, "that you don't have to get sick and suffer. If you live sensibly you can have health and energy for many years. Above all, reprogram your mind. Everything starts in the mind."

3. *Live in the present.* One of the temptations of the older generation is to retreat into "the good old days." Pleasant memories

are fine, but the way to keep young is to think youthfully, looking forward and not back. Our responsibilities and opportunities are *now*. Unless we forget the past, as Paul did (Philippians 3:13), we cannot enjoy the gifts and tasks God has for us here and now.

I don't like the word *retirement*. I suggest you substitute for it in your thinking the word *readjustment*. No one should retire from life! Retirement is an opportunity to readjust your life so you can think new thoughts, do new things, see new places, and form new friendships. Develop the habit of concentrating on the present and planning for the future, and you will always be young in heart.

4. *Set yourself some worthy goals.* A friend of mine advised his son, "If you don't aim at something, you won't hit anything." That is true for everyone. The happiest people I know, of any age, are those who have new goals on their horizons.

Here in Pawling, New York, Dr. Ralph Lankler spent many years as pastor of Christ Church on Quaker Hill. Toward the end of his active ministry, he and his neighbor John Brown, both well past retirement age, formed an interfaith ministry in which the churches of the village work together to provide food, medical aid, and other assistance for anyone in the community needing help. It has been remarkably successful.

5. *Exercise faith in your heavenly Father.* Dr. William Barclay, looking back over his life, said of the golden years:

> Surely the years will bring an increasing conviction of the triumphant adequacy of the grace of God. When we look back on life, we see all that we have come through in the way of sorrow and tears, of pain and of toil; and we know that we would not be on our own two feet today were it not for God's grace. The experience of the past must give confidence for the future.
>
> The advice is . . . "Grow old with wisdom and with God, sure that the best is yet to be."

Guideposts magazine recently told of a bedridden woman in a nursing home who wondered what she could do for someone else. Looking out her window at a skyscraper under construction, she began to pray for the workers' safety. She was thrilled that after the men learned of her prayers, they sent her a hard hat signed with all their names. Although there were some accidents during the building of the skyscraper, no one was killed or badly injured. And this remarkable lady learned that there is always something worthwhile a person can do—bringing blessings to oneself as well as to others.

6. *Fill your life with joy.* When you focus on the positive, happy aspects of your life, you tend to multiply those. Remember that a "merry heart" is like medicine (Proverbs 17:22) and that "the joy of the Lord is your strength" (Nehemiah 8:10).

For those who love and laugh and believe, the sunset years are not cold or gray but warm and golden with the presence of God. And while we grow in years, we can remain young and vigorous in spirit—and in mind and body too.

Another ingredient of healthful well-being is having friends, which I will discuss in the next chapter.

For good health and long life:

1. Familiarize yourself with the great Bible passages that recount the health-giving power of the Lord.
2. Practice the principles and precepts of wholesome living.
3. Maintain positive, healthful attitudes.
4. Pray and live in the spirit of Jesus and of the Bible's teaching.
5. Approach old age hopefully and expectantly.
6. Live in the present and plan for the future; never get bogged down in the past.
7. Set yourself worthy goals and work toward them.

ARE YOU LONELY?

A best-selling book years ago bore the unusual title *Everybody's Lonesome*. The main idea, as I recall, was that everyone is looking for a friend, and that we can find friends galore if we keep that fact in mind. For everyone, deep down, is searching for genuine friendship and love.

And friends are very important for our well-being. In her "Personal Health" column in the *New York Times* on February 5, 1992, Jane Brody wrote:

> Friendship, immortalized in literature, song and aphorism, is increasingly being recognized as vital to health and happiness.
>
> In study after study, medical researchers have found that people who have friends they can turn to for affirmation, empathy, advice, and assistance as well as for affection are more likely to survive health challenges like heart attacks and major surgery and are less likely to develop diseases like cancer and respiratory infections.

The Bible recognizes the importance of friends. God knew that "It is not good that . . . man should be alone" (Genesis 2:18). It reminds us how friends can help us: "A friend loveth at all times, and a brother is born for adversity" (Proverbs 17:17). "Faithful are the wounds of a friend" (Proverbs 27:6). A true friend, that is, may inadvertently hurt our feelings, but she or he acts and speaks for our good.

Finding Friends

The Bible contains some very important information about finding friends. First, the person "that hath friends must show himself friendly" (Proverbs 18:24). Nothing important happens without effort. If you want a friend, are you willing to become a friend? Have you acquired negative habits or mannerisms or attitudes that put people off?

Think about people you like. Why do you like them? Isn't one reason the fact that they take an interest in other people and are genuine in their attitude toward everyone?

Act aloof and you will be alone. Be friendly and you will find friends. Find interesting things to talk about. Take a genuine interest in the person you want to befriend.

And don't let unimportant things end a good friendship. Like a good marriage, a friendship is a continuing work of art. Work at your friendships, and work at deepening them. As the wise writer of Proverbs counsels, "Thine own friend . . . forsake not . . . for better is a neighbor that is near than a brother far off" (27:10).

Who in the Bible had the most friends? Besides Jesus, surely the apostle Paul would make a good candidate for that distinction. All over the civilized world he had friends who gave him a home away from home, who supported him in his many troubles, and who hugged him and wept inconsolably when they feared they would see him no more (Acts 20:37–38).

Paul would probably not be the easiest person in the world to live with. He had an unbending allegiance to the Lord and to His truth as he saw it. But he gave of himself without limit for Christ and for everyone he could persuade to accept His love. And Paul was a profound encourager. From the thirteen letters of his in the New Testament we can see that he knew how to befriend and persuade: He always began with positive encouragement. After that, as necessary, Paul tried to correct what needed correction, but always in the spirit of love and goodwill.

Perhaps the supreme encourager of the Bible was Barnabas. When the disciples were afraid of Paul because of his previous crusade against them, it was Barnabas, whose name means "son of encouragement," who brought him to the apostles (Acts 9:27). After Paul retreated to Tarsus, it was Barnabas who brought him back into the church (Acts 11:25–26). And later, when Paul had no more use for young John Mark, it was Barnabas who stood by the youth's side, apparently encouraging him back into the Lord's work (Acts 15:36–39).

Study the Bible's examples. Interest yourself in other people, love them, bear with them, encourage them, and you will win friends.

Image Yourself No Longer Lonely

A woman who would have been attractive if she had not let her unhappiness mar her features once lamented, "I'm so lonely I just want to die." Talking with her, I found that she had a mental image of herself locked up in a prison of that loneliness.

"Do you know who holds the key to your prison cell?" I asked her.

"No," she answered with a puzzled look, "not really."

"I think you do know," I told her. "The key is your picture of yourself. I challenge you to throw that picture away and substitute this one: See yourself as the outgoing, friendly, attractive person you really are and can be. Make a mental image of a new you, doing things other people like to do, inviting a friend to lunch, remembering someone's birthday, reaching out to someone else who is lonely. Hold that image before you and make a real effort to be a friend to at least one person. And ask God for the help He wants to give you. Prayerize. Visualize. Actualize. And you will break completely out of that prison of loneliness."

The change didn't happen all at once, but this woman is working at her new self-image, and she is far busier and happier, and she already has more friends.

Follow the same suggestions and you will be happier and even healthier.

You Have a Friend

You already have one friend who can do you more good than you can imagine. "There is a friend that sticketh closer than a brother" (Proverbs 18:24). Who is that friend?

Three of the most important words ever written are: "God is love" (1 John 4:8). If you ever feel lonely or depressed or discouraged, think about that great fact.

Think of the whole Bible as God's great Love Letter to us. The first page tells with what tender, loving care He made the world—for us "to have dominion over"—to care for, to preserve, and to enhance. Everything on earth He made for our good (Genesis 1:26–31).

In particular, the Lord made you and us and all His children in His image and likeness (Genesis 1:26). Why? Evidently He loved to commune with the first man and woman "in the cool of the day" (Genesis 3:8). And when Adam and Eve disobeyed Him, it broke His heart. For their own good they had to be disciplined, but He promised that a redeemer would come. That redeemer, who would be attacked by the serpent but would destroy it (Genesis 3:15), is our Savior. We are promised in Romans 16:20 that through Christ, "The God of peace shall bruise Satan under your feet."

The Bible records God's desire to have fellowship with His children in every age. Enoch walked with Him. God told His dreams and plans to Noah, Abraham, Isaac, Jacob, Joseph, Moses, and those in every age who took time to listen to Him. He wants us for His special friends!

And the Bible tells us that His love for each one of us is just like a parent's love for his child . . . or a man's love for his bride . . . or the matchless companionship of a good friend (Psalm 103:13; Ephesians 5:25; John 15:15).

June Masters Bacher once wrote in *Daily Guideposts* of receiving a mysterious greeting the day before Valentine's Day. It was a card surrounded by forget-me-nots addressed to "A Special Friend." The unsigned card said: "Just another chance to tell you in secret what you have meant in my life."

You can imagine what a lift June received from that loving, anonymous note. And all through the Bible God puts little notes of love to inspire us to be our best and reach our highest goals.

Much of the Bible is in the form of letters. The Gospel of Luke and its continuation in Acts are letters from Luke to a friend named Theophilus (Luke 1:3; Acts 1:1). Most of the New Testament consists of thirteen letters from Paul and other letters from James, Peter, John, and Jude. The last book of the Bible, Revelation, begins with seven letters from Jesus to seven churches in Asia Minor (modern Turkey).

Each of these letters—and every part of the Bible—is a message of love from the Supreme One who has us in His heart.

> **God is well able to love each one of us
> as though we were the only person in the universe.**

If you feel lonely, turn to some of the great passages that reveal God's special love for you. Write them down, repeat them, and let them warm your heart. Here are a few of His love notes:

The Lord your God which goeth before you, he shall fight for you (Deuteronomy 1:30).

Be strong and of a good courage; be not afraid, neither be thou dismayed: for the Lord thy God is with thee whithersoever thou goest (Joshua 1:9).

Thou wilt show me the path of life: in thy presence is fullness of joy (Psalm 16:11).

Wait on the Lord: be of good courage, and he shall strengthen thine heart (Psalm 27:14).

I have loved thee with an everlasting love: therefore with loving-kindness have I drawn thee (Jeremiah 31:3).

With God nothing shall be impossible (Luke 1:37).

God so loved the world that he gave his only begotten Son (John 3:16).

Who shall separate us from the love of Christ? (Romans 8:35).

The God of love and peace shall be with you (2 Corinthians 13:11).

We love him, because he first loved us (1 John 4:19).

With all the people in this vast world, you may wonder how God could have a special love for you. But God made the world! He is infinitely greater than we can imagine. He is well able to love each one of us as though we were the only person in the universe.

John and Charles Wesley were two of eighteen children. Yet their mother made time to spend an hour every week individually with each child, just as though that child were the only one she had.

John Wesley became a remarkable Christian leader, traveling eight thousand miles a year on horseback and eventually renewing the whole church. His brother Charles wrote over five thousand hymns, many of which we still sing.

The self-esteem Susannah Wesley built into her children produced two spiritual geniuses. And God is pouring out His love for you just as though you were His only child.

Since God loves you so much, relax in His love. Pamper yourself a little today. Is there some special food you like? Some special activity you enjoy? Take time today to experience it, and your heavenly Father will rejoice in your joy.

Then sit down for a few moments and try to feel the sunlight of God's love coursing through your body, warming your heart, invigorating your mind, renewing every fiber of your being. Repeat over and over: "God is Light. God is Life. God is Love." Relax in the loving presence of your Father in heaven.

Take the loving presence of God with you into the next thing you do, into your contact with the next person you meet. You will have a very good day!

The knowledge of God's love is what everyone needs. Anne Brooks of Tampa, Florida, was crippled with arthritis when she volunteered to help in a health clinic. There an osteopathic physician helped ease her pain and also encouraged her to believe that she could get better. Gradually she overcame her immobility and then trained to become a physician herself. Today she is the only doctor in a tiny village in Mississippi. "I get much more from people here than I could ever give them," she says. In finding and sharing the power of God's love she has found the joyous reality of abundant life.

The Lord will bless you as you receive His love and share it with someone else.

Three Great Facts

There are three wonderful facts that, when understood and spiritually assimilated, can work wonders in your life. They are three of the greatest truths of the Bible.

1. *God is for you.* Many people feel that life is against them. They have a chip on their shoulder and spend their days complaining about the unfairness of things in general.

Well, life doesn't always seem fair. Again and again, when something bad happens, we ask, "Why?" Circumstances may pile up against us. Friends may turn against us. Everything may seem to be going wrong.

When the poet Robert Browning wrote, "God's in his heaven, all's right with the world," he was telling only half the real truth. God is in heaven, but everything is not yet right with the world! We only need read the day's news to be reminded of that.

Whatever happens, however, God wants you to know that He is for you. When Abraham was surrounded by moon-worshiping pagans in ancient Haran, God assured him that He was for him: "I will bless thee, and make thy name great" (Genesis 12:2). When Jacob was on his way home in fear of the uncle and brother he had cheated, "the angels of God met him" (Genesis 32:1) and let him know that God stood for him despite his sins. After Joseph had been sold into slavery and then was imprisoned, God raised him up to one of the highest positions in Egypt. When Moses, desperate to save his people from slavery, was eighty years old and must have felt about ready to give up his dream, God appeared in a burning bush with the message that He was about to work wonders for Moses and his fellow Israelites.

On and on through the Bible goes the record of God's assurance in every generation that He is for us, on our side, with a love that will never let us go. "We know that all things work together for good to them that love God" (Romans 8:28). These words may also be translated "We know that in everything God works for good with those who love him" (RSV). Isn't that wonderful? Whatever happens, God is in it with us, working everything out *for our good!*

Corrie ten Boom used to illustrate this by holding up a piece of knitting, wrong side out. From the underside one sees only a jumble of twisted ends and colors. But from the upper side a beautiful design is visible.

Life may often look like the underside of that knitting, twisted and seemingly meaningless. But if we thoughtfully view it from the upper side, we will be able to see the beautiful pattern God has been weaving in our lives.

Romans 8:31 asks, "If God be for us, who can be against us?" It continues, "He that spared not his own Son, but delivered him up for us all, how shall he not with him also freely give us all things?" (verse 32).

An unusual wedding took place recently out of doors in Pawling, New York. The bridegroom supervises the maintenance of a complex of ponds, waterways, and plantings designed for maximum ecological benefit. The wedding ceremony was held in a gazebo built by the groom near a small stream, surrounded by wildflowers. During the service, in the midst of the traditional liturgy, he and his bride each read vows they had written personally in their own words to express their commitment. Although each statement was different, each contained the expression "I will be here for you."

God wants each of us to know that He is here *for us.* Just as a good friend always stands by us and encourages us and works for us, so our Father in heaven stands by to help us.

A young black man became completely discouraged by all the hurts and difficulties he had met. He talked about it with his pastor, however, until his discouragement was gone. This is how he described that visit: "All the stars had gone out of my sky. One by one the minister put every star back into the sky."

God does that for us. When we feel down and out, He puts all the stars back in our sky and renews our spirits. Over and over in the Bible He says, as He does in Ezekiel 36:9, "Behold, I am for you."

2. *God is with you.* Our Lord does not simply look on from afar and wish us well. He is right here with us in all we do.

Jesus' name Emmanuel means "God with us" (Matthew 1:23). God encourages us, "Fear not: for I am with thee" (Isaiah 43:5). Jesus promised, "Lo, I am with you always, even unto the end of the world" (Matthew 28:20).

One of the retirees from the Peale Center entered a two-mile charity benefit race in the New England village where he lives. When his son-in-law (who runs in the New York marathon) learned of his plans, he became a little anxious about his aging father-in-law's well-being. So he too entered the race and ran alongside him.

"His presence there was so encouraging," our ex-employee reported, "that I made the best time of my life, and I won the over-sixty prize!"

The word "comforter" in John 14:16 means one who stands by, encourages, and helps. It may refer to the Greek citizen who ran alongside a soldier going to battle, encouraging him on. So God is with us, beside us in our needs, helping and encouraging.

3. *God is in you.* I have often observed that the word *enthusiasm* means "God within." A believer is not half-dead or half-hearted! He or she is enthusiastic because God is Life and Christ came to bring us life in all its vibrant abundance. And God is in us if we believe.

The Lord wants to fill us completely with His presence and power and joy and hope. Jesus said, "Without me you can do nothing" (John 15:5). But with Him inwardly strengthening us we can do everything we need to do (Philippians 4:13). Christ in us is our hope (Colossians 1:27).

Gideon was just a discouraged Israelite when the Philistines swept through the Promised Land, ravaging the countryside. But the angel of the Lord came to him while he was at work and promised to use him to drive out those hated invaders. You can read the whole fascinating story in Judges chapters 6 through 8.

Early in his military campaign it is recorded that "the Spirit of the Lord came upon Gideon" (Judges 6:34). Those words in the original Hebrew, scholars tell us, mean that "the Spirit of the Lord clothed Himself with Gideon."

The Lord wants to clothe Himself with us. Without Him we are like scarecrows, stuffed with the rags of our own self-doubt, self-importance, and self-righteousness. If He fills us with His Spirit, we can fight the good fight of faith in His love and power, with confidence and victory.

The Book of Zephaniah contains prophecies of destruction, but it concludes with this sunburst of hopefulness: "The Lord thy God in the midst of thee is mighty; he will save, he will rejoice over thee with joy; he will rest in his love, he will joy over thee with singing" (3:17). In other words, God is not only with us and in our midst, but He is so proud of what we are and what we can be that He rejoices over us with songs of delight!

This is what God is and does. He comes into our lives and rejoices over us just as we are, and over the majestic potential He sees in us.

Write these three great affirmations on a card and carry it with you, repeating every day:

> God is for me.
> God is with me.
> God is in me.

Try this experiment: As you read the Bible, mark the additional verses you find that remind you of these truths. And underline in your Bible this great promise:

> When thou passest through the waters,
> I will be with thee; and through the rivers,
> they shall not overflow thee:
> when thou walkest through the fire,
> thou shalt not be burned; neither shall the flame
> kindle upon thee.
>
> Isaiah 43:2

Repeat these great words until you know them by heart. They will fill your life with strength and joy.

Never Alone

A friend of mine grew tired of the responsibilities of being a minister in a suburban New York church. He took the pastorate of a tiny church in upstate New York with the longish name of Nevin Memorial United Presbyterian Church. He discovered that it had been founded by a remarkable minister named John Nevin.

Nevin was a bachelor who had been born in Ireland. Coming to a farming area in New York State where there was no church, he walked from door to door and became an indispensable friend of everyone he contacted. Over the years he built up a congregation who responded to his patient faithfulness and love, and eventually he founded a new church. After his death it was appropriately remembered by his name.

One of the members once asked, "Pastor Nevin, don't you ever get lonely, living all by yourself?" "No," answered John Nevin, "I'm never alone! It's me and the Savior together, and a wonderful time we have of it."

And you will have a wonderful time every day of your life if you let God hold you tight.

You need never be lonely if you:

1. Make the effort to have friends.
2. Imagine yourself no longer lonely. Prayerize, visualize, and actualize until the image becomes reality.
3. Picture God loving you as though you were His unique child, as indeed you are.
4. Read the Bible as the love letter it is, from God to you.
5. Repeat to yourself the Bible's assurances of God's boundless love.
6. Pamper yourself a little now and then. Take time to enjoy God's love gifts.
7. Remember that God is for you, God is with you, and God is in you.
8. Share God's love with someone else, and make new friends through Him.

SUCCESS SECRETS OF THE BIBLE

13

*P*eople who succeed greatly are impressive, especially when they overcome immense odds in the process. *Guideposts* magazine often tells the stories of such people, and the Horatio Alger Awards often honor such individuals.

The idea of success is often viewed disparagingly because it may seem materialistic. And the word *success* appears only once in the King James Bible. But equivalent terms such as *blessing* and *prosperity* are often found, and the idea of succeeding is an important scriptural concept.

Success is reaching your potential. God wants us to do what we are able to do in the world. It is the person who lives primarily for others who achieves true success.

So none of us should be content to fail or only half succeed at what we do. The Bible's heroes of faith are indeed heroes: winners, "more than conquerors." They accomplished remarkable victories. If Abraham had not succeeded in his trek from Babylonia to Palestine, if Moses or Gideon or John or Paul or any of the Bible's key individuals had failed in their mission, vital links would have been broken, and you and I might very well have never met the Master. At the end of His life Jesus could say of His work, "It is finished"

(John 19:30); Paul could say at the end of his, "I have fought a good fight, I have finished my course, I have kept the faith" (2 Timothy 4:7). And by God's grace every believer will be able to say the same.

I like what Phillips Brooks, a noted New England preacher and poet, said: "To find his place and fill it is success for a man." And the great statesman Charles Malik put it well: "Success is neither fame, wealth, nor power; rather, it is seeking, knowing, loving, and obeying God. If you seek, you will know; if you know, you will love; if you love, you will obey."

Ralph Waldo Emerson said that success means:

To laugh often and love much
To win the respect of intelligent persons and the affection of
   children
To earn the appreciation of honest critics
To endure the betrayal of false friends
To appreciate beauty
To find the best in others
To leave this world a little bit better whether by a healthy
   child, a garden patch, or a redeemed social condition
To know even one life has breathed easier because you have
   lived—this is to have succeeded.

Real success is the spiritual process of developing a mature and constructive personality through which a person can accomplish his or her highest objectives with the help of God.

The Elements of Success

What are the most important characteristics for success?

In more than fifty years as a pastor I have baptized a good many babies, and adults too. It is a great privilege to bring a human being before God in Christian dedication. Sometimes during a baptism I have asked myself, "If I had the power, what values would I instill into this life?" Here is my answer: the qualities of Christian character—confidence, enthusiasm, courage, honesty, persistence, and an outgoing spirit of love and joy. And above all, faith. For faith is the spring from which all the other qualities flow.

These characteristics, of course, are among those most vital to success in any endeavor. They were central to the successes recorded in the Bible, and they bring success today—in our spiritual growth, and in the rest of life too.

1. *Confidence.* Success is impossible without confidence. When Amelia Earhart was a little girl she had the confident, optimistic look on her face that endeared her to so many Americans as the First Lady of Aviation. Throughout her life, she believed she could do the impossible—and she broke one flying record after another.

Confidence is faith in yourself, resulting from faith in God. It is freedom from uncertainty, unhappiness, and the fear of failure. Abraham Lincoln once said, "It is difficult to make a man miserable while he feels he is worthy of himself and claims kindred to the great God who made him."

The models of faith in the Bible did not always begin their work with confidence. Moses felt he was unequal to the task of freeing his people. Gideon refused to begin his mission until he had put out a fleece to get the Lord's confirmation. But God encouraged both men until they had enough self-confidence to succeed. He wants to encourage you in the same way. And He urges, "Cast not away your confidence" (Hebrews 10:35).

A man once told me that after he had heard me preach at Marble Collegiate Church he didn't remember a word of my sermon. Fortunately, he did remember something far more important—my text. It was "I can do all things through Christ who strengthens me," (Philippians 4:13 NKJV). The man said, "I was having a very hard time. I repeated those words over and over. They built up my confidence and renewed my life."

They will build up your confidence too. Here are some more confidence builders:

All things are possible to him that believeth (Mark 9:23).
I will not fail thee, nor forsake thee (Joshua 1:5).
God is our refuge and strength, a very present help in trouble (Psalm 46:1).
My God shall supply all your need according to his riches in glory by Christ Jesus (Philippians 4:19).
You are the light of the world (Matthew 5:14 RSV).

2. *Enthusiasm.* Is it possible to accomplish anything without enthusiasm? I do not believe so. Enthusiasm comes from the words *en theos*, "God within." It means giving yourself completely to something. And while you will not find this word in the Bible, you will find a good equivalent: zeal.

The Bible enthusiastically recommends enthusiasm:

> My zeal hath consumed me (Psalm 119:139).
>
> Whatsoever thy hand findeth to do, do it with thy might (Ecclesiastes 9:10).
>
> Not slothful in business; fervent in spirit; serving the Lord (Romans 12:11).
>
> It is good to be zealously affected always in a good thing (Galatians 4:18).
>
> Whatsoever ye do, do it heartily, as to the Lord, and not unto men (Colossians 3:23).
>
> Above all things have fervent charity among yourselves (1 Peter 4:8).

My friend Eric Fellman, editor-in-chief at the Peale Center for Christian Living, told me recently of his dismay during one of his first winters in Pawling, New York. The gutters on his house filled with ice, melting snow backed up under the roof, and the ceilings began leaking.

Eric got out a ladder and climbed up to the gutters while his three small sons watched curiously. First he tried to melt the ice with rock salt. Nothing happened. Then he hacked away at the ice with a hammer and chisel. Finally he used a propane torch, but nothing could get rid of that ice.

What saved the day was hot water. Eric hooked a garden hose to the water heater, and in just a few minutes the scalding water melted all the ice.

Eric, who knows the Bible so well that I constantly marvel, said that the situation reminded him of Revelation 3:15. There the Lord intimates that He prefers a fire-eyed fanatic or a stone-cold unbeliever to a lukewarm, unenthusiastic half-believer. Where lukewarm water would have done no good, and might well have made the situation worse, hot water did the trick. And where lukewarmness accomplishes nothing, the fire of enthusiasm works wonders.

3. *Courage.* Courage is another essential of a good life and of success. When the Israelites stood at the edge of the Promised Land, Moses encouraged them with these words: "Be strong and of a good courage, fear not, nor be afraid . . . for the Lord thy God, he it is that doth go with thee; he will not fail thee, nor forsake thee" (Deuteronomy 31:6).

Any venture requires courage. Whatever we do, we can do it without fear if we remember these words. For if God is with us, who or what can stand against us?

Of course none of us is so brave that we are never fearful at all. A degree of fear can save life. To stand at the edge of a skyscraper or close to an express train with no fear whatever is a mark more of foolishness than of courage. I never address an audience without a measure of trepidation. But to be overwhelmed by fear is also foolish. Someone has said, and said truly, that courage is not so much the absence of fear as going ahead in spite of our fears.

Think of the courage of Abraham, leaving his home and family to travel a thousand miles into unknown territory. Or of Moses when he faced down the seemingly omnipotent power of the pharaoh who ruled Egypt. Or of Joseph when he defied the seductions of Potiphar's wife. Or of Daniel looking into a den of hungry lions.

Our problems today are usually less dramatic, but the kingdom of God marches forward because of the same kind of courage on the part of millions of outwardly ordinary men and women.

In 1914 a poor eight-year-old named Soichiro Honda watched a Ford Model T sputter down the street of the Japanese village where his father tried to earn enough money as a blacksmith to feed his large family. When he was fifteen, with little education, Soichiro looked for a job as an auto mechanic. Soon afterward he started his own repair shop, branching out into making bicycles and then motorcycles. After Honda motorcycles became a worldwide success, Soichiro decided to start building automobiles.

Here he ran afoul of his country's industrial bureaucracy. They decided that Japan needed only a few auto manufacturers and ordered him to keep making motorcycles only. But, defying the bureaucrats, Honda built one of the most successful auto companies in history. It would never have happened if Soichiro Honda,

like Henry Ford and many other innovative businesspeople, had
not had the courage of his convictions.

That same kind of courage is needed today, whatever we do. And
we will possess invincible courage if we listen to God's Word:

> We may boldly say, The Lord is my helper, and I will not fear what
> man shall do unto me (Hebrews 13:6).
> Be of good courage, and do it (Ezra 10:4).

4. *Honesty.* Although there is no question that honesty is the best
policy, as Cervantes said, the sad fact is that we live in a world
where half-truths and semideceptions often tempt us to be less than
our best. Yet God always blesses honesty. He promises:

> He that walketh righteously, and speaketh uprightly;
> he that despiseth the gain of oppressions, that shaketh
> his hands from holding of bribes . . . He shall dwell on high:
> his place of defense shall be the munitions of rocks:
> bread shall be given him; his waters shall be sure.

> Isaiah 33:15–16

In other words, if we walk resolutely in honest paths, if we keep
our words honest, and refuse even to think of anything that smacks
of bribery or dishonest gain, we will have the best security there
is, the favor of God.

In the sixth chapter of this book I wrote quite a bit about honesty. Let me close this section by recounting a true story that was
in the news recently.

Tracy Wilson, a twenty-seven-year-old single mother of three,
was earning $2.10 an hour when she found a large sum of money.
Just before Christmas, she was given some used clothes. When she
took them home she discovered in the pocket of a robe a stack of
bills totaling one thousand dollars. A not inconsiderable amount
when you have no money in the bank! But badly as she needed
money, Tracy values honor more. She returned the money to the
donor of the clothing.

When Tracy was asked why she didn't just keep the money, she
said, "It wasn't mine to keep." Then some neighbors who learned

what had happened got together and collected a donation for her. It nearly equaled the thousand dollars she had returned.

5. *Persistence.* The Bible's word for this vital quality is faithfulness or patience. It tells us that God "will render to every man according to his deeds: To them who by patient continuance in well doing seek for glory and honor and immortality, eternal life" (Romans 2:6–7). But those who do not persist in the spiritual climb can expect only trouble and anguish (verses 8 and 9).

One of the most outstanding characteristics of men and women of faith is their persistence in doing well. Abraham, Joseph, Moses, David, Isaiah, Daniel, and the apostles had many important qualities, but if they had not kept on we would never have heard of them. Of course, some of them faced such difficulties that they temporarily failed—as we all do at times. Peter vowed to be true to Jesus always and then denied that he even knew Him. But he picked himself up and started over. That is the essence of persistence. Always pick yourself up and start again!

Bible scholars tell me that the word for *faith* in the New Testament grows straight out of the word *faithfulness* in the Old Testament. And the Scriptures are insistent about the importance of keeping the faith, holding fast, never giving up. Some examples are Luke 18:1; Galatians 6:9–10; Hebrews 2:1–3; Hebrews 10:38–39. Paul urges with all the force of his being: "having done all . . . stand" (Ephesians 6:13).

A president of Wheaton College in Illinois, Dr. V. Raymond Edman, put it well: "The last dejected effort often becomes the winning stroke."[1] Henry Ford, asked how a young person could become successful, answered in seven words: "If you start a thing, finish it."[2] It is said of the legendary basketball player Larry Bird, "He never quits."

One of America's financial wizards is John Templeton, whose mutual funds have enjoyed unusual success. In 1952 Templeton helped found the Young Presidents' Organization. Each of the members of this group, from all parts of the world and all kinds of backgrounds, became president of a good-sized company before he was forty. Templeton says that the one thing these talented but diverse individuals have in common is perseverance. "When they undertake to accomplish something, they accomplish it," he wrote in the *International Christian Digest.* "The program may change along the way, but they don't give up."

John Templeton believes that certain principles are "as important for our welfare as stopping for a red light at a busy intersection." He calls them the Laws of Life. They include humility, enthusiasm, truthfulness, joy, reliability, faithfulness, and perseverance. He says of the latter: "You will always give your business and your trust to someone who will see a project through even if difficulties arise—and they usually do."[3]

6. *The spirit of love and joy.* There are two basic ways to live. One is the immature, self-indulgent way of life described in Galatians 5:19–21. In looking for happiness, you never find it.

The other way is that described in Galatians 5:22–23. It is the Christian way. And its first two characteristics are love and joy. That is the kind of life I would like to see everyone have.

In the Holy Land there are two lakes. One is called the Sea of Galilee. For thousands of years it has been a delightful lake; today fishermen still catch fish there, just as they did in the days of Jesus.

The other lake, a little to the south, is the Dead Sea. It is formed by the same River Jordan that feeds Galilee. But its waters are so bitter and brackish that nothing can live either in it or near it. It is truly a dead sea.

The same water supplies both these lakes. What is the difference? The only difference is that Galilee has an outlet while the Dead Sea has none. The Jordan's waters flow into Galilee and out again, and the lake is always fresh and pleasant. The Dead Sea, being below sea level, has no outlet; the only way its waters leave is by evaporation. And when they evaporate, they leave salt and other chemicals behind, resulting in increasing bitterness.

As wiser persons than I have noticed, right there in Palestine is a living parable of the two basic ways of life. The outgoing person receives love and passes it on. The self-centered person hoards what he gets and everything turns bitter and poisonous. You have observed both types of people. Which are you? Which would you like to be? Jesus came so that anyone could become the first type, loving and happy and successful.

7. *Faith.* This may seem like something static, something you either have or don't have. Actually, in the Bible faith (like love) is an action word. To have faith in God is to begin the most exciting adventure in the world. When you read the Gospels, notice how often Jesus calls for a specific action as a mark of faith. "Arise," He said to a paralyzed man, "take up thy bed, and go unto thine house" (Matthew 9:6). He told a man with a crippled hand to stretch it forth, and as he did it was healed (Mark 3:5). When He called the apostles, He sent them out to perform works like His own (Matthew 10:1–8).

We walk by faith (2 Corinthians 5:7) and we live by faith (Romans 1:17). God tells us to fight the good fight of faith (1 Timothy 6:12), and in that fight faith is a shield that protects the heart (Ephesians 6:16).

The Letter to the Hebrews emphasizes how vital faith is. Without faith it is impossible to please God (Hebrews 11:6). Faith brings hope to reality and helps us see the invisible things of the spiritual world (Hebrews 11:1). Through faith we understand (Hebrews 11:3), and by faith Abel, Noah, Abraham, and numerous others accomplished marvelous things.

Faith is instinctive. When you sit down, you exercise faith that the chair will hold you. You don't need a lot of faith to accomplish something; Jesus said that if we have faith like a grain of mustard seed (one of the tiniest seeds on earth), we can move mountains, and "nothing will be impossible" (Matthew 17:20).

So use the faith you have. Like anything else, faith is strengthened by use. Build up your faith by reading the Bible, doing what it says, associating with people of faith, praying, and exercising your faith constantly in positive Christian living.

One great American who radiated these vital qualities—confidence, enthusiasm, courage, honesty, perseverance, love, joy, and faith—was Louis Klopsch, who originated the red-letter Bible and founded the Christian Herald organization in this country. Beginning life with nothing, eventually he helped feed numerous victims of earthquakes, floods, and famines in many parts of the world and was honored by three American presidents and by leaders of other countries. Those who knew him said he always worked "with all his might." Charles Pepper wrote of Klopsch: "He believed, with all the strength of his forceful nature, that the Lord prospers every really good work that is undertaken for His sake." Irving Bacheller said, "His religion was full of joy . . . He fought the good fight with a brave and merry heart . . . He loved little children, especially those of the poor, and his chief recreation was drawn from the happiness that he gave them."[4]

These same characteristics are true of so many people I have met that I must say with the writer of Hebrews (11:32), "the time would fail me to tell" of them all. They describe the true positive thinker.

These seven qualities together form a bridge so strong that it will carry you over any difficulty. With adequate confidence you will make the best possible beginning in any venture. With enthusiasm, courage, and perseverance you are bound to win. With love and faith and the other characteristics outlined here, you have the foundation for success in your life journey, in business or whatever you do.

J. C. Penney and Joshua

James Cash Penney, like many of America's great businessmen, began life as a very poor boy. His farmer father was so hard pressed financially that before James was twelve, he told him that henceforth he would have to earn his own clothes.

James did it. Growing up the hard way, eventually he produced one of our best known chains of stores. Originally he called the Penney stores "Golden Rule Stores" because he had made Christ's Golden Rule the main principle of his business as well as his life.

Although Mr. Penney had a number of ups and downs, his faith was always strong. After many years in business he said: "My parents ingrained in me their faith in God, and the belief that right always triumphs eventually . . . It seems to me that anyone inclined to question whether one can be a business success and a good Christian at one and the same time need look for reassurance no further than to the words spoken by the Lord to Joshua, when He bade him lead the children of Israel across the river Jordan into the land which was to be their home."

What were God's words to Joshua? You will find them in the first chapter of the Book of Joshua, verses 7 and 8:

Only be thou strong and very courageous, that thou mayest observe to do according to all the law, which Moses my servant commanded thee: turn not from it to the right hand or to the left, that thou mayest prosper whithersoever thou goest.

This book of the law shall not depart out of thy mouth; but thou shalt meditate therein day and night, that thou mayest observe to do according to all that is written therein: for then thou shalt make thy way prosperous, and then thou shalt have good success.

Study these words carefully for an understanding of some of the basic principles through which God grants "good success."

A Strategy for Success

The Christians of the first century A.D. must have sometimes felt listless and low, for the Book of Hebrews urges them not to be "wearied and faint in your minds" (Hebrews 12:3). The same passage exhorts: "Wherefore lift up the hands which hang down, and the feeble knees" (Hebrews 12:12). A tired person's hands droop and his knees do not want to propel his legs. Such a condition is a sad one.

What is the remedy? This great twelfth chapter of Hebrews begins with a striking picture of a race. The setting is a stadium filled with a vast "cloud" of witnesses—the men and women of faith mentioned in chapter 11. These earlier heroes surround us, urging us to "run with patience the race that is set before us" (verse 1). They have run their own races and won; now they encourage each of us to press on in our individual life journeys.

But the key words are "Looking unto Jesus, the author and finisher of our faith" (verse 2). The Scottish theologian James Stewart says that "looking unto Jesus" means three things: Look out and not in; look up and not down; look forward and not back.

Look Out and Not In

Probably it is valuable to examine ourselves once in a while. But there is such a thing as too much introspection. The Bible constantly cautions us to look for our salvation not to ourselves but to our Savior, "on whom faith depends from start to finish" (Hebrews 12:2 NEB). "For by grace are ye saved through faith; and that not of

> **If you look too much within yourself, you can reinforce failure patterns from the past. Instead, look beyond yourself and concentrate on your goal.**

yourselves: it is the gift of God: not of works, lest any man should boast" (Ephesians 2:8–9).

Ancient Job, wracked with sickness, found health and blessing when he stopped lamenting his misfortunes and began praying for his friends (Job 42:10–11).

After an astounding victory over the child-sacrificing priests of Baal, the prophet Elijah fell into fearful despondency, insisting that he alone remained faithful to God (1 Kings 19:9–10). Depression and other negative attitudes always distort reality. The Lord had to remind him that there were at least seven thousand others in Israel who loved God (verses 14–18). At the same time He gave the prophet a new vision and new orders. After this simple and sensible explanation, Elijah received new energy to continue God's work.

The application? If you look too much within yourself, you can reinforce failure patterns from the past. Instead, look beyond yourself and concentrate on your goal. Picture yourself succeeding, and you will.

Look Up and Not Down

I once heard of a man who, as a child, found some loose change on the ground. Thereafter he kept looking for money. Forty years later he had acquired 2,713 pennies, 358 nickels, 210 dimes, 76 quarters, 9 fifty-cent pieces, 2 silver dollars, and a bent back.

An unknown individual has written:

> Two men looked out through prison bars.
> The one saw mud; the other, stars.

When God wanted to encourage Abraham, He took him out under the night sky and told him to look at the stars. The upward look reminds us, among other things, of what is valuable because it is permanent.

Looking down, we can see the unfinished business of what is and has been. That can be discouraging. Looking up, we can visualize what can be and will be if we help make it so. That means hope and renewed energy.

A modern painting portrays Jesus sitting on a hillside overlooking a lake. He is looking up, smiling, as He communes with His Father. Our Lord spent a great deal of time among men and women with needs and problems. But the Gospels reveal that He also spent much time in prayer (Matthew 14:23; Mark 1:35; Luke 5:16; 9:18; 11:1).

And the Bible tells us that to win the race of life we must look not to ourselves but to God and to Jesus, "the author and finisher of our faith" (Hebrews 12:2). He is the beginning, the end, and the center of our spiritual journey. He who "hath begun a good work in you will perform it until the day of Jesus Christ" (Philippians 1:6).

Look Forward and Not Back

Satchel Paige was a wise athlete. He once remarked, "Don't look back. Somethin' may be gainin' on you." He had a good point! While it may be useful occasionally to review the past, we must not dwell there. Jeremiah records God's lament that His people, instead of listening to Him and walking in His ways, "went backward, and not forward" (Jeremiah 7:24). Someone has said that the Seven Last Words of the Church are "We never did it this way before."

The Savior did not succeed by concentrating on what He had already done. Rather, He "for the joy that was set before him endured the cross" (Hebrews 12:2). Looking forward to the joy of succeeding, He endured the agony of His sufferings and crucifixion.

Paul knew this principle well. "Forgetting those things which are behind," he wrote, "and reaching forth unto those things which are before, I press toward the mark for the prize" (Philippians 3:13–14). And we are to do likewise: "Let us therefore . . . be thus minded" (verse 15). God's call to us is to look ahead, think ahead, plan ahead, and win.

John Templeton was once asked how he succeeded so well in the mutual funds he oversees so effectively. He answered, "We are looking ahead to the bull market after the next one." Some experts say that one reason Germany and Japan have done so well commercially is that they deliberately plan for a successful future. Certainly it is the forward look that is a vital ingredient of success.

When sixteen-year-old Toni Nieminen brought Finland and his fellow skiers two gold medals for his record ski jumps in the 1992 Winter Olympics, he said to a reporter, "I believed we could do it." And his faith produced victory.

How the Class Dunce Rose to the Top

One of my dearest friends is Homer Surbeck, one of Wall Street's smartest, most successful, and best loved lawyers. But as Homer tells it, he started school as the class dunce. He was nearsighted and a bit shy. His first-grade teacher in Lead, South Dakota, finally gave up trying to instruct him, he recalls, and sent him home with a note that said in effect: "This boy tries hard, but he is so slow I can't teach him anything."

Now Homer had a wonderful father. On seeing the note, he said to Homer, "If your teacher can't teach you, you will have to teach yourself. You can do it. And when you have learned to teach yourself, you won't need a teacher."

Then Homer's father taught him how to go over and over a lesson until he knew it. Homer discovered that if he kept at it, he *could* do it. Next, he learned to review each previous lesson before starting a new one. The process was so effective that he began to study with enthusiasm, and from the third grade on Homer Surbeck was always at the top of his class. He graduated with honors from engineering school, got a scholarship to the law school of Yale University, and graduated there at the top of his class. This qualified him for appointment as law clerk to William Howard Taft, chief justice of the United States Supreme Court. Then he served for over fifty years with the prestigious legal firm of Hughes, Rounds, Schurman & Dwight, headed by Charles Evans Hughes. Among Homer's many awards is the Yale Medal, the highest honor given by the Association of Yale Alumni.

Homer Surbeck's life was not without problems, of course. When he got to high school, he found that he did not have time to go over all his lessons as he had done before. At this point his mother gave him an insight that has marked his life ever since.

1. *Receptivity to divine guidance* is the first principle in what Homer calls "the success formula that really works." When his mother learned of his difficulty in high school, she told him: "Pray for guidance about what is most important in each lesson. Then give your time first to what is most important."

Homer followed her advice and found that it worked splendidly. Throughout his life he has let God tell him what is important and has concentrated on that. He has discovered that these words from Psalm 16:7 apply today: "I will bless the Lord who counsels me; he gives me wisdom in the night. He tells me what to do" (LB).

"When I seek God's help," says Homer, "relax, and wait with patience, the answer always comes."

2. *Honest best efforts with enthusiasm* is the way Homer Surbeck describes the second principle of success. When he was a child his father gave him a coaster wagon which he loved to ride in—particularly when another boy pushed! But to be pushed, he found that he had to take turns pushing his partner while the other boy steered.

Homer says he found that if he pushed with secret resentment, pushing the wagon was terrible drudgery and the other child didn't appreciate the ride. But if he pushed someone else with enthusiasm simply to make him happy, it became such fun that the other boy usually insisted on pushing him even farther!

This, he found, is what the Golden Rule teaches us. If we treat others the way we would like to be treated, they will give back what we gave them, and often even more.

Give your honest best effort to whatever you do, with enthusiasm, and your rewards will be great.

3. *Focusing on a noble purpose* is the third principle in Homer's formula. Proverbs 3:6 promises, in the Living Bible's paraphrase: "In everything you do, put God first, and he will direct you and crown your efforts with success." Honoring God and seeking always to do His will means finding a noble cause and doing your part to accomplish it.

4. *Being useful beyond oneself* is Homer's final success principle. He says this was driven home to him when he applied for his first job after law school. He had what he thought were two great interviews with Emory Buckner, the head of an eminent legal firm.

You can imagine Homer's surprise when Buckner said, "I don't want you." Buckner explained that during the whole two hours they had talked, the subject had been what the firm could do for Surbeck, not what he could do for it.

It would have been easy to feel totally crushed when Buckner added, "Get out!" But Surbeck sent up a quick prayer: "What do I do now?" And "the answer came right back clear and strong," he says. He sincerely thanked Mr. Buckner for such valuable advice. And when he applied to Charles Evans Hughes for the job he really wanted most, he concentrated on making known what he could contribute. Shifting from his own interests to a purpose beyond himself got him the job—and lifted him from rung to rung on the ladder of success.

Jesus said, "Seek ye first the kingdom of God, and his righteousness; and all these things [that are needed] shall be added unto you" (Matthew 6:33).

What are your hopes and plans and goals? Think them through, commit them to God, and He will grant you good success.

To become all you were meant to be:

1. Believe that you can measure up to the potential God has put within you.
2. Build up your confidence through affirmations such as this: "I can do all things through Christ who strengthens me."
3. Do everything you do with enthusiasm.
4. Practice the art of courage.
5. Be absolutely honest in every situation.
6. Learn from successful individuals, in the Bible and elsewhere.
7. Build good habits into your daily life.
8. Be receptive to God's guidance.
9. Commit your goals to God, your Creator and Friend.

*N*ow It's Your Turn

*W*e have examined the Bible from Genesis to Revelation and found it is full of power for everyday living. There is only one way to have this power for yourself—you must dig into the Word of God and make its truths real in your life.

When you read the Bible every day, you will find that it gives you something new at each sitting, for "the Word of God is quick [alive], and powerful" (Hebrews 4:12).

So take this ancient command to heart and find for yourself the strength, hope, and health the Bible offers:

> And these words, which I command thee this day, shall be in thine heart: and thou shalt teach them diligently to thy children, and shalt talk of them when thou sittest in thine house, and when thou walkest by the way, and when thou liest down, and when thou risest up.
>
> Deuteronomy 6:6–7

Additional inspirational reading is available in Dr. Peale's booklet How to Make Jesus Your Best Friend. For your free copy, write to: PEALE CENTER FOR CHRISTIAN LIVING, 66 E. MAIN STREET, PAWLING, N.Y. 12564.

$\mathcal{N}$OTES

Introduction

1 Norman Vincent Peale, *The Power of Positive Thinking*. Prentice Hall, 1952, v.
2 *The Power of Positive Thinking*, 120.

Chapter One: Happier, Healthier Living

1 "Terry Anderson Looks Back . . ." *New York Times International*, March 15, 1992, 10.
2 Rex Kern, *Guideposts*, October 1969, 13.
3 Stanley Ford, *What the Bible Tells the Businessman* (pamphlet), Peale Center for Christian Living.
4 Svetlana Alliluyeva, *Only One Year*. Harper & Row, 1969, 296.
5 For a free copy of *Thought Conditioners* or *Spirit Lifters* write to Peale Center for Christian Living, 66 East Main Street, Pawling, NY 12564–1409.

Chapter Two: How to Tackle a Giant Problem

1 From the videotape "Pain and Healing" in the series *The Mind*, copyright by the Educational Broadcasting Corporation.

Chapter Three: Move Up out of the Darkness

1 Agnes Sanford, "The Healing of Memories." *Guideposts*, November 1969.
2 *Daily Guideposts 1987*, devotion for April 10.

Chapter Four: Have a Good Day Every Day

1 Dr. Raj K. Chopra, *Making a Bad Situation Good*. Thomas Nelson Publishers, 1984, 30–40, 45.
2 John Oxenham, *Bees in Amber*. Revell, 1959, 61.
3 Helen Steiner Rice, *Mothers Are a Gift of Love*. Revell, 1980, 36.

Chapter Five: The Way to Lasting Happiness

1 C. S. Lewis, *Letters to Malcolm*. Harcourt, Brace & World, 1964, 95.

Chapter Six: Three Keys to Personal Freedom

1 Ruth Carter Stapleton, *The Experience of Inner Healing*. Word, 1977, 183–85.

Chapter Eight: The Power of Hope

1 *New York Times*, December 24, 1991, science section, 1.
2 Steven Locke and Douglas Colligan, *The Healer Within*. Dutton, 1986, 192–93.
3 *Newsweek*, July 4, 1989, 35.
4 Gerald L. Coffee, *Beyond Survival*. G. P. Putnam's Sons, 1990, 278–79.
5 Alan Loy McGinnis, *The Power of Optimism*. HarperCollins, 1990, passim.

Chapter Nine: Multiply Your Blessings

1 Lane Adams, *Plus: The Magazine of Positive Thinking* (published by the Peale Center for Christian Living), March 1985, 26–36.

Chapter Ten: A Sure Cure for Fear and Stress

1 *Northeast* magazine, September 13, 1990, 9–18.
2 S. I. McMillen, *None of These Diseases*. Revell, 1984, 109–15.

3 John Greenleaf Whittier, "The Eternal Goodness."
4 William Barclay, *The New Testament: A New Translation*, Volume 1. Collins, 1968, 333.
5 Mildred Leightner, "Safe Am I."
6 Horatio Spafford, "It Is Well with my Soul."

Chapter Eleven: God's Way to Good Health and Long Life

1 *None of These Diseases*, 12–17.
2 Osler and Ishigami quotes in *The Healer Within*, 60–61.
3 Bernard S. Siegel, *Love, Medicine and Miracles*. Harper & Row, 1986, 6.
4 Harris Dienstfrey, *Where the Mind Meets the Body*. HarperCollins, 1991, 125, 132–33.
5 Lewis Thomas, *A Long Line of Cells*. Book of the Month Club, 1990, 64.
6 *Letters of William James*. Henry James, ed. Atlantic Monthly Press, 1920, Vol. I, 146–47.
7 Dr. Ben H. Douglas, *AgeLess*. QRP Books, 1990, 115, 180.
8 Dr. Linus Pauling, *How to Live Longer and Feel Better*. W. H. Freeman and Co., 1986, 227.
9 Andrew Goliszek, *Breaking the Stress Habit*. Carolina Press, 1987, 132.
10 E. Stanley Jones, *A Song of Ascents*. Abingdon, 1968, 335–39.

Chapter Thirteen: Success Secrets of the Bible

1 Dr. V. Raymond Edman, *The Disciplines of Life*. Van Kampen Press, 1948, 140.
2 *The Disciplines of Life*, 138.
3 "Templeton's Laws of Life," *International Christian Digest*, February 1988, 35–36.
4 Charles M. Pepper, *Life-Work of Louis Klopsch*, The Christian Herald, 1910, vii, 347, 354–57, passim.